ISBN 978-1-333-79565-8
PIBN 10551238

This book is a reproduction of an important historical work. Forgotten Books uses
state-of-the-art technology to digitally reconstruct the work, preserving the original format
whilst repairing imperfections present in the aged copy. In rare cases, an imperfection in
the original, such as a blemish or missing page, may be replicated in our edition. We do,
however, repair the vast majority of imperfections successfully; any imperfections that
remain are intentionally left to preserve the state of such historical works.

1 MONTH OF
FREE
READING

at
www.ForgottenBooks.com

By purchasing this book you are eligible for one month membership to ForgottenBooks.com, giving you unlimited access to our entire collection of over 1,000,000 titles via our web site and mobile apps.

To claim your free month visit:
www.forgottenbooks.com/free551238

ROMAN JAKOBS

MORRIS HALLE

Fundamentals
of
Language

FUNDAMENTALS OF LANGUAGE

JANUA LINGUARUM

STUDIA MEMORIAE
NICOLAI VAN WIJK DEDICATA

edenda curat

CORNELIS H. VAN SCHOONEVELD
LEIDEN

NR. I

1956
MOUTON & CO · 'S-GRAVENHAGE

UNDAMENTALS OF LANGUAGE

by

ROMAN JAKOBSON
HARVARD UNIVERSITY

and

MORRIS HALLE
MASSACHUSETTS INSTITUTE OF TECHNOLOGY

1956

MOUTON & CO · 'S-GRAVENHAGE

Printed in the Netherlands by
Mouton & Co., Printers, The Hague

FOREWORD

The GATE OF LANGUAGES (*Janua linguarum*) is indeed an appropriate title for a series of essays seeking the key to the laws that govern language and its relationship with other social institutions. This name appeals to me, moreover, as a link that connects the modern search with the writings of Johann Amos Comenius, the great humanist thinker in the science of language. His works, like many Greek and Latin treatises from the Stoa to the Cartesian epoch, carry numerous fruitful ideas which now again capture the attention of linguists.

The title of the series refers, furthermore, to the recent past of our science. Nicolaas van Wijk, whose name heads this set of essays, was one of the outstanding pioneers in the inquiry into the structure of language and into the principles of its evolution. The subtitle of his book *Phonologie* – "een hoofdstuk uit de structurele taalwetenschap" (a chapter of structural linguistics) – may be applied to his whole life's work. In 1902, as a twenty-two year old student at Leipzig, he offered a bold contribution 'Zur relativen Chronologie der urgermanischen Lautgesetze', published in Paul-Braune *Beiträge zur Geschichte der deutschen Sprache und Literatur*, XXVIII, in which he displays a clear insight into the coherence of sound patterns and their mutations, and some twenty years later he took up and elaborated these views in his first original work in comparative phonology, 'Een phonologiese parallel tussen Germaans, Slavies en Balties', *Mededeelingen der Koninklijke Akademie van Wetenschappen*, Afd. Letterkunde, deel 77–79, serie A (1934–5). Van Wijk, and there lies his main strength, never sacrificed the manifold empirical data in favor of a speculative theory, nor did his amazing mastery of the concrete philological material conceal from him the theoretical corollaries.

I am particularly glad to inaugurate the series of essays dedicated to the memory of this eminent Dutch linguist, since twenty five years ago it was he who, along with Antoine Meillet, encouraged my first, modest attempts to grasp the structural laws of language with respect to the factors of time and space (*De nieuwe taalgids,* XXIV, XXV). It is again to the author of *Phonologie* (1939) that I feel deep gratitude for the first support of my initial efforts to dissolve language into its ultimate components, the dyadic distinctive features.

When a quarter of a century separates us from the Prague International Conference, which broke the ground for general phonology, it is appropriate to survey the main problems of this discipline in its present stage. On the other hand, it was tempting to explore, forty years after the publication of Saussure's *Cours* with its radical distinction between the "syntagmatic" and "associative" plane of language, what has been and can be drawn from this fundamental dichotomy.

Leiden, October 1955　　　　　　　　　　ROMAN JAKOBSON

TABLE OF CONTENTS

PART II

TWO ASPECTS OF LANGUAGE AND
TWO TYPES OF APHASIC DISTURBANCES

SUPPLEMENT

The first study is an expanded version of the paper to appear in the *Handbook of Phonetics*, initiated by the International Committee for Phonetic Sciences and prepared for publication by the North Holland Publishing Company, Amsterdam. The second study is based on the author's essay written for a collective volume *At the Beginning Was the Word*, Harper, New York, and on a few passages of his paper "Aphasia as a Linguistic Problem" from the symposium *On Expressive Language*, Clark University Press, Worcester, Mass., 1955.

PART I

PHONOLOGY AND PHONETICS

BY

ROMAN JAKOBSON

AND

MORRIS HALLE

THE FEATURE LEVEL OF LANGUAGE

1.1 *Distinctive features in operation.* Family names such as *Bitter, Chitter, Ditter, Fitter, Gitter, Hitter, Jitter, Litter, Mitter, Pitter, Ritter, Sitter, Titter, Witter, Zitter,* all occur in New York. Whatever the origin of these names and their bearers, each of these vocables is used in the English of New Yorkers without colliding with their linguistic habits. You had never heard anything about the gentleman introduced to you at a New York party. "Mr. Ditter," says your host. You try to grasp and retain this message. As an English-speaking person you, unaware of the operation, easily divide the continuous sound-flow into a definite number of successive units. Your host didn't say *bitter* /bitə/ or *dotter* /dátə/ or *digger* /digə/ or *ditty* /diti/ but *ditter* /dítə/. Thus the four sequential units capable of selective alternation with other units in English are readily educed by the listener: /d/+/í/+/t/+/ə/.

Each of these units presents the receiver with a definite number of paired alternatives used with a differentiating value in English. The family names, cited above, differ in their initial unit; some of these names are distinguished from each other by one, single alternative, and this minimal distinction is common to several pairs, e.g. /nitə/:/ditə/ = /mitə/: /bitə/ = nasalized *vs.* non-nasalized; /títə/:/dítə/ = /sítə/:/zítə/ = /pitə/:/bitə/ = /kítə/:/gítə/ = tense *vs.* lax. Such pairs as /pitə/ and /ditə/ offer an example of two concurrent minimal distinctions: grave *vs.* acute together with tense *vs.* lax. The pair *bitter* /bitə/ and *detter* /détə/ presents two successive minimal distinctions: grave *vs.* acute followed by diffuse *vs.* compact. For an acoustic and motor definition of the cited distinctions, see 3.61 and 3.62.

1.2 *Structure of distinctive features.* Linguistic analysis gradually breaks down complex speech units into morphemes as the ultimate constituents endowed with proper meaning and dissolves these minutest semantic vehicles into their ultimate components, capable of differentiating morphemes from each other. These components are termed distinctive features. Correspondingly, two levels of language and linguistic analysis are to be kept apart: on the one hand, the semantic level involving both simple and complex meaningful units from the morpheme to the utterance and discourse and, on the other hand, the feature level concerned with simple and complex units which serve merely to differentiate, cement and partition or bring into relief the manifold meaningful units.

Each of the distinctive features involves a choice between two terms of an opposition that displays a specific differential property, diverging from the properties of all other oppositions. Thus grave and acute are opposed to each other in the listener's perception by sound-pitch, as relatively low-pitched and high-pitched; in the physical aspect they are correspondingly opposed by the distribution of energy at the ends of the spectrum and on the motor level by the size and shape of the resonating cavity. In a message conveyed to the listener, every feature confronts him with a yes-no decision. Thus he has to make his selection between grave and acute, because in the language used for the message both alternatives occur in combination with the same concurrent features and in the same sequences: /bitə/—/dítə/, /fitə/—/sítə/, /bil/—/búl/. The listener is obliged to choose either between two polar qualities of the same category, as in the case of grave *vs.* acute, or between the presence and absence of a certain quality such as voiced *vs.* voiceless, nasalized *vs.* non-nasalized, sharp *vs.* plain.

1.3 *Opposition and contrast.* Since in the listener's hesitation "Is it /bitə/ or /dítə/?" only one of the two logically correlated alternatives belongs to the actual message, the Saussurian term opposition is suitable here, whereas the term contrast is rather to be confined to cases where the polarity of two units is brought into relief by their contiguity in sensory experience as, for instance, the contrast of grave and acute in the sequence /pi/ or the same contrast, but with a reversed order of features, in the sequence /tu/. Thus opposition and contrast are two different manifestations of the polarity principle and both of them perform an important role in the feature aspect of language (cf. 3.4).

1.4 *Message and code.* If the listener receives a message in a language he knows, he correlates it with the code at hand and this code includes all the distinctive features to be manipulated, all their admissible combinations into bundles of concurrent features termed phonemes, and all the rules of concatenating phonemes into sequences – briefly, all the distinctive vehicles serving primarily to differentiate morphemes and whole words. Therefore, the unilingual speaker of English, when hearing a name like /zítə/ identifies and assimilates it without difficulty even if he had never heard it before, but either in perception or reproduction he is prone to distort, and to distrust as alien, a name such as /ktítə/ with its unacceptable consonantal cluster, or /xítə/ which contains only familiar features but in an unfamiliar bundle, or, finally, /mýtə/, since its second phoneme has a distinctive feature foreign to English.

1.5 *Ellipsis and explicitness.* The case of the man faced with family names of people entirely unknown to him was deliberately chosen because neither his vocabulary, nor his previous experience, nor the immediate context of the conversation give him any clues for the recognition of these names. In such a situation the listener can't afford to lose a single phoneme from the message received. Usually, however, the context and the situation permit us to disregard a high percentage of the features, phonemes and sequences in the incoming message without jeopardizing its comprehension. The probability of occurrence in the spoken chain varies for different features and likewise for each feature in different texts. For this reason it is possible, from a part of the sequence, to predict with greater or lesser accuracy the succeeding features, to reconstruct the preceding ones, and finally to infer from some features in a bundle the other concurrent features.

Since in various circumstances the distinctive load of the phonemes is actually reduced for the listener, the speaker, in his turn, is relieved of executing all the sound distinctions in his message: the number of effaced features, omitted phonemes and simplified sequences may be considerable in a blurred and rapid style of speaking. The sound shape of speech may be no less elliptic than its syntactic composition. Even such specimens as the slovenly /tem mins sem/ for 'ten minutes to seven', quoted by D. Jones, are not the highest degree of omission and fragmentariness encountered in familiar talk. But, once the necessity arises, speech that is elliptic on the semantic or feature level, is readily translated by the utterer into an explicit form which, if needed, is apprehended by the listener in all its explicitness.

The slurred fashion of pronunciation is but an abbreviated derivative from the explicit clear-speech form which carries the highest amount of information. For many American English speakers /t/ and /d/ are ordinarily not distinguished between a stressed and unstressed vowel but can be produced distinctively when there is danger of a confusing homonymity: "Is it Mr. Bitter /bitə/ or Bidder /bídə/?" may be asked with a slightly divergent implementation of the two phonemes. This means that in one type of American English the code distinguishes the inter-vocalic /t/ and /d/, while in another dialectal type this distinction is totally lost. When analyzing the pattern of phonemes and distinctive features composing them, one must resort to the fullest, optimal code at the command of the given speakers.

THE VARIETY OF FEATURES
AND THEIR TREATMENT IN LINGUISTICS

2.1 *Phonology and phonemics.* The question of how language utilizes sound matter, selecting certain of its elements and adapting them to its various ends, is the field of a special linguistic discipline. In English this discipline is often called p h o n e m i c s (or, puristically, p h o n e m a t i c s) since among the functions of sound in language the primary one is to serve as a distinctive vehicle and since the basic vehicle for this function is the phoneme with its components. The prevailingly continental term p h o n o l o g y (launched in 1923 and based on the suggestions of the Geneva school),[1] or the circumlocution f u n c t i o n a l p h o n e t i c s is to be preferred however, although in English the label "phonology" frequently designated other domains and especially served to translate the German *Lautgeschichte.* The advantage of the term "phonology" might be its easier application to the whole variety of linguistic functions performed by sound, whereas "phonemics" willy-nilly suggests a confinement to the distinctive vehicles and is an appropriate designation for the main part of phonology dealing with the distinctive function of speech sounds.

While phonetics seeks to collect the most exhaustive information on gross sound matter, in its physiological and physical properties, phonemics, and phonology in general, intervenes to apply strictly linguistic criteria to the sorting and classification of the material registered by phonetics. The search for the ultimate discrete differential constituents of language can be traced back to the *sphoṭa*-doctrine of the Sanskrit grammarians[2] and to Plato's conception of στοιχεῖον, but the actual linguistic study of these

---

[1] R. Jakobson, *O češskom stixe* (Berlin, 1923), pp. 21ff.

[2] Cf. J. Brough, 'Theories of general linguistics in the Sanskrit Grammarians,' *Transactions of the Philosophical Society* (1951).

invariants started only in the 1870's and developed intensively after
World War I, side by side with the gradual expansion of the principle
of invariance in the sciences. After the stimulating international
discussion of the late twenties and early thirties, the first attempts
to sum up the basic results of the research, Trubetzkoy's and van
Wijk's outlines of general phonology, appeared in 1939.[3] The subsequent theoretical and practical achievements in the structural
analysis of language required an ever more adequate and consistent
incorporation of speech sounds into the field of linguistics with its
stringent methodology; the principles and techniques of phonology
improve and its scope becomes ever wider.

2.2 *The "inner" approach to the phoneme in relation to sound.*
For the connection and delimitation of phonology (especially
phonemics) and phonetics, the crucial question is the nature of the
relationship between phonological entities and sound. In Bloomfield's conception, the phonemes of a language are not sounds
but merely sound features lumped together "which the speakers
have been trained to produce and recognize in the current of speech
sounds – just as motorists are trained to stop before a red signal,
be it an electric signal-light, a lamp, a flag, or what not, although
there is no disembodied redness apart from these actual signals."[4]
The speaker has learned to make sound-producing movements in
such a way that the distinctive features are present in the sound
waves, and the listener has learned to extract them from these waves.
This so-to-speak inner, immanent approach, which locates the
distinctive features and their bundles within the speech sounds, be
it on their motor, acoustical or auditory level, is the most appropriate premise for phonemic operations, although it has been
repeatedly contested by outer approaches which in different ways
divorce phonemes from concrete sounds.

2.3 *Types of features.* Since the differentiation of semantic units
is the least dispensable among the sound functions in language,

---

[3] N. Trubetzkoy, 'Grundzüge der Phonologie' = *Travaux du Cercle
Linguistique de Prague*, VII (1939); N. van Wijk, *Phonologie: een hoofdstuk
uit de structurele taalwetenschap* (The Hague, 1939).
[4] L. Bloomfield, *Language* (New York, 1933), p. 79f.

speech participants learn primarily to respond to the distinctive features. It would be deceptive, however, to believe that they are trained to ignore all the rest in speech sounds. Beside the distinctive features, there are, at the command of the speaker, also other types of coded information-bearing features that any member of a speech community has been trained to manipulate and which the science of language has no right to disregard.

Configurative features signal the division of the utterance into grammatical units of different degrees of complexity, particularly into sentences and words, either by singling out these units and indicating their hierarchy (culminative features) or by delimiting and integrating them (demarcative features).

Expressive features (or emphatics) put the relative emphasis on different parts of the utterance or on different utterances and suggest the emotional attitudes of the utterer.

While the distinctive and the configurative features refer to semantic units, these two types of features, in turn, are referred to by the redundant features. Redundant features help to identify a concurrent or adjoining feature, either distinctive or configurative, and either a single one or a combination. The auxiliary role of redundancies must not be underestimated. Circumstances may even cause them to substitute for distinctive features. Jones cites the example of the English /s/ and /z/ which in final position differ from each other solely in the degree of breath force. Although "an English hearer will usually identify the consonants correctly, in spite of their resemblance to one another," the right identification is often facilitated by the concomitant difference in the length of the preceding phoneme: *pence* [peñs] – *pens* [pen:z].[5] In French, the difference between voicelessness and voicing ordinarily accompanies the consonantal opposition tense/lax. Martinet notes that in an energetic shout the lenis /b/ matches the fortis /p/ in energy so that a strong *bis!* differs from *pisse!* only through the normally redundant feature voiceless/voiced.[6] Conversely, in Russian, the difference between lax and tense is a redundant feature accompany-

---

[5] D. Jones, *The Phoneme: its nature and use* (Cambridge, 1950), p. 53.
[6] *Word*, XI (1955), p. 115. Cf. R. Jakobson, C. G. M. Fant, M. Halle,

ing the distinctive opposition voiced/voiceless, while under the special conditions of whispering only the redundant feature remains and takes over the distinctive function.

If the distinctive function of speech sounds is the only one under analysis, we use the so-called "broad" or phonemic transcription, that notes nothing but phonemes. In a Russian specimen /pil,íl/ '(one) spread dust', /i/ is an unstressed phoneme that includes, furthermore, two distinctive features: in traditional articulatory terms, /i/ is opposed to /a/ of /pal,íl/ '(one) fired' as narrow to wide and to /u/ of /pul,ál/ '(one) took a pot shot' as unrounded to rounded. The information load of the vowel analyzed is, however, far from confined to its distinctive features, notwithstanding their paramount relevance in communication.

The first vowel of /pil,íl/ is a velar [ɯ] in contradistinction to the palatal [i] of /p,il,íl/ '(one) sawed' and this difference between back and front is a redundant feature pointing to the distinctive opposition of the preceding unpalatalized (plain) and palatalized (sharp) consonant: cf. Russian /r,áp/ 'pitted' – /r,áp,/ 'ripple'.

If we compare the sequences /krugóm pil,il/ '(one) spread dust all around' and /ispómpi l,il/ '(one) poured from a pump', we observe that the syllable /pi/ in the second specimen contains a more obscure (tending toward a brief, mid-central articulation) variety of vowel than in the first sample. The less obscure variety appears only immediately before the stressed syllable of the same word and thus displays a configurative feature: it signals that no word boundary follows immediately.

Finally, /pil,íl/ may be uttered with a prolongation of the first, pretonic vowel [ɯ:] to magnify the narrated event, or with a prolongation of the second, accented vowel [í:] to imply a burst of emotion.

The velarity in the first vowel of /pil,íl/ denotes the antecedent plain feature; the unreduced, less obscure character denotes that no word boundary follows; the vowel lengthening denotes a certain

---

Preliminaries to speech analysis, third printing (Massachusetts Institute of Technology, Acoustics Laboratory, 1955), p. 8.

kind of emphasis. Possession of a single specific denotation unites the redundant features with the configurative and expressive features and separates them from the distinctive features. Whatever distinctive feature we tackle, the denotation is always identical: any such feature denotes that the morpheme to which it pertains is not the same as a morpheme having another feature in the corresponding place. A phoneme, as Sapir remarked, "has no singleness of reference."[7] All phonemes denote nothing but mere otherness. This lack of individual denotation sets apart the distinctive features, and their combinations into phonemes, from all other linguistic units.

The code of features used by the listener does not exhaust the information he receives from the sounds of the incoming message. From its sound shape he extracts clues to identify the sender. By correlating the speaker's code with his own code of features, the listener may infer the origin, educational status and social environment of the sender. Natural sound properties allow the identification of the sex, age, and psychophysiological type of the sender and, finally, the recognition of an acquaintance. Some ways to the exploration of these physiognomic indices were indicated in Siever's *Schallanalyse*,[8] but their systematic study still remains on the agenda.

2.41 *The "outer" approaches to the phoneme in relation to sound: A. The mentalist view.* An insight into the complexity of the informational content of speech sounds is a necessary premise for the discussion of the various outer approaches to the phoneme in its relation to sound. In the oldest of these approaches, going back to Baudouin de Courtenay and still surviving, the phoneme is a sound imagined or intended, opposed to the emitted sound as a "psychophonetic" phenomenon to the "physiophonetic" fact. It is the mental equivalent of an exteriorized sound. The unity of

---

[7] E. Sapir, 'Sound patterns in language,' *Selected Writings* (Berkeley and Los Angeles, 1949), p. 34.

[8] See especially E. Sievers, 'Ziele und Wege der Schallanalyse,' *Festschrift für W. Streitberg* (Heidelberg, 1924).

the phoneme, as compared with the variety of its implementations, is seen as a discrepancy between the internal impetus aiming at the same pronunciation and the involuntary vacillation in the fulfillment.

This conception is based on two fallacies: we have no right to presume that the sound correlate in our internal speech or in our speech intention is confined to the distinctive features to the exclusion of the configurative, or redundant features. On the other hand, the multiplicity of contextual and optional variants of one and the same phoneme in uttered speech is due to the combination of this phoneme with diverse redundant and expressive features; this diversity, however, does not hamper the extraction of the invariable phoneme from among all these variations. Thus the attempt to overcome the antinomy between invariance and variability by assigning the former to the internal and the latter to the external experience distorts the two forms of experience.

2.42   *B. The code-restricting view.* Another attempt to locate the phoneme outside the uttered sounds confines the phonemes to the code and the variants to the message. A rejoinder to this view would be that the code includes not only the distinctive features, but also the redundant and configurative features which induce contextual variants as, well as the expressive features which underlie optional variations: the users of a language have learned to effect and apprehend them in the message. Thus phoneme and variants alike are present, both in the code and in the message.

A cognate tenet, advanced especially in Russia, opposed the phoneme to the variants as social value to individual behavior. This is hardly justifiable since not only the distinctive features but all the coded features are equally socialized.

2.43   *C. The generic view.* Phoneme has frequently been opposed to sound as class to specimen. It has been characterized as a family or class of sounds related through a phonetic resemblance. Such definitions, however, are vulnerable in several respects.

First, the vague and subjective search for resemblance must be replaced by the extraction of a common property.

Second, both the definition and the analysis of the phoneme must take into account the logical lessòn that "classes can be defined by properties, but it is hardly possible to define properties by classes." [9] In fact, when operating with a phoneme or distinctive feature we are primarily concerned with a constant which is present in the various particulars. If we state that in English the phoneme /k/ occurs before /u/, it is not at all the whole family of its various submembers, but only the bundle of distinctive features common to all of them, that appears in this position. Phonemic analysis is a study of properties, invariant under certain transformations.

Third, when dealing with a sound that in a given language figures in a definite position, under definite stylistic conditions, we are again faced with a class of occurrences and their common denominator, and not with a single, fleeting specimen. Whether studying phonemes or contextual variants ("allophones"), it is always, as the logician would say, the "sign-design" and not the "sign-event" that we define.

2.44   D. The fictionalist view. According to the opinion most effectively launched by Twaddell in 1935,[10] but latently tinging writings of various authors, phonemes are abstractional, fictitious units. As long as this means nothing more than that any scientific concept is a fictional construct, such a philosophical attitude cannot affect phonemic analysis. Phoneme, in this case, is a fiction, in the same way as morpheme, word, sentence, language, etc. If, however, the analyzer opposes the phoneme and its components to sound as a mere contrivance having no necessary correlate in concrete experience, the results of the analysis will be distorted through this assumption. The belief that the choice among phonemes to which we assign the sound might, upon occasion, be made arbitrarily, even at random, threatens the objective value of phonemic analysis. This danger may, however, be avoided by the

---

[9]   R. Carnap, *Meaning and necessity* (Chicago, 1947), p. 152.
[10]   W. F. Twaddell, 'On defining the phoneme' = Supplement to *Language*, XVI (1935); cf. M. J. Andrade, 'Some questions of fact and policy concerning phonemes,' *Language*, XII (1936).

methodological demand that any distinctive feature and, consequently, any phoneme treated by the linguist, have its constant
correlate at each stage of the speech event and thus be identifiable
at any level accessible to observation. Our present knowledge of
the physical and physiological aspects of speech sounds is sufficient
to meet this demand. The sameness of a distinctive feature throughout all its variable implementations is now objectively demonstrable.
Three reservations, however, must be made.

First, certain features and combinations of features may be
obliterated in the various kinds of phonemic ellipsis (cf. 1.5).

Second, features may be masked by abnormal, distorting conditions of sound production (whispering, shouting, singing, stam-
mering), transmission (distance, filtering, noise) or perception
(auditory fatigue).

Third, a distinctive feature is a relational property so that the
"minimum same" of a feature in its combination with various
other concurrent or successive features lies in the essentially
identical relation between the two opposite alternatives. However
the stops in *tot* may differ from each other genetically and acoustically, they are both high-pitched in opposition to the two labials in
pop, and both display a diffusion of energy, as compared to a
greater concentration of energy in the two stops of *cock*. How
the sameness of a phoneme in two divergent contextual variants is
sensed by the speakers, may be illustrated by such onomatopoetic
sound reduplications as *cack, kick, tit, peep, poop*.

2.441 *"Overlapping" of phonemes*. The so-called overlapping of
phonemes confirms the manifestly relational character of the
distinctive features. A pair of palatal vowel phonemes, genetically
opposed to each other through relative wideness and narrowness
and, acoustically, through a higher and lower concentration of
energy (compact/diffuse), may in some languages be implemented
in one position as [æ] – [e] and in another position as [e] – [i],
so that the same sound [e] in one position implements the diffuse,
and in another, the compact term of the same opposition. The
relation in both positions remains identical. Two degrees of aperture

and, correspondingly, of concentration of energy – the maximal and the minimal – oppose each other in both positions.

The focusing of selective operations upon relational properties is typical not only of human, but even of animal behavior. In W. Koehler's experiment, chickens were trained to pick grain from a gray field and to leave the grain untouched on the adjacent darker field; when, subsequently, the pair of fields, gray and dark, was replaced by a pair, gray and light, the chickens looking for their food left the gray field for its lighter counterpart. Thus "the chicken transfers its response to the relatively brighter area."[11] It is first of all through the relational rules that the listener guided by the linguistic code apprehends the message.

2.45   *E. The algebraic view.* The approach one might call "algebraie" aims at the maximal estrangement between phoneme and sound or, correspondingly, between phonemics and phonetics. The champion of this trend, Hjelmslev, calls on linguistics to become "an algebra of language, operating with unnamed entities, i.e. arbitrarily named entities without natural designation".[12] Particularly, the "expression plane" of language, as he christened the aspect named *signans* in Stoic and Scholastic tradition, and in the work of its reviver Ferdinand de Saussure, is to be studied without any recourse to phonetic premises.

Each venture, however, to reduce language to its ultimate invariants, by means of a mere analysis of their distribution in the text and with no reference to their empiric correlates, is condemned to failure. The comparison of two English sequences – /ku/ and /uk/ – will yield no information on the identity of the first segment in one of these samples with the second segment in the other sample, unless we bring into play sound properties common to initial and final /k/ and those common to /u/ in both positions. The con-

[11]   See H. Werner, *Comparative psychology of mental development* (New York-Chicago-Los Angeles, 1940), p. 216f.

[12]   L. Hjelmslev, 'Prolegomena to a theory of language' = *Indiana University Publications in Anthropology and Linguistics*, VIII (1935), p. 50; cf. the objective criticism of this approach by B. Siertsema, *A study of glossematics* ('s-Gravenhage, 1954), chapters VI, XI, and by F. Hintze, 'Zum Verhältnis der sprachlichen "Form" zur "Substanz",' *Studia Linguistica*, III (1949).

frontation of the syllables /ku/ and /ki/ does not authorize us to assign both initial segments to one phoneme /k/ as two variants appearing to their mutual exclusion before two different vowels, unless we have identified the common features, unifying the retracted and advanced variety of the phoneme /k/ and differentiating it from all other phonemes of the same language. Only through such a test are we able to decide whether the retracted [k-] in /ku/ implements the same phoneme as the advanced [k+] in /ki/ and not the advanced [g+] in /gi/. Therefore, despite the theoretical requirement of an analysis totally independent of the sound substance, in practice "on tient compte de la substance à toute étape de l'analyse", as Eli Fischer-Jørgensen exposes the troubling discrepancy.[13]

As to the theoretical requirement itself, it arose from the assumption that in language form is opposed to substance as a constant to a variable. If the sound substance were a mere variable, then the search for linguistic invariants would indeed need to expunge it. But the possibility of translating the same linguistic form from a sound substance into a graphic substance, e.g. into a phonetic notation or into an approximately phonemic spelling system does not prove that the sound substance, like other "widely different expression substances", is a mere variable. In contradistinction to the universal phenomenon of speech, phonetic or phonemic writing is an occasional, accessory code that normally implies the ability of its users to translate it into its underlying sound code, while the reverse ability, to transpose speech into letters, is a secondary and much less common faculty. Only after having mastered speech does one graduate to reading and writing. There is a cardinal difference between phonemes and graphic units. Each letter carries a specific denotation – in a phonemic orthography, it usually denotes one of the phonemes or a certain limited series of phonemes, whereas phonemes denote nothing but mere otherness (cf. 2.3). Graphic signs that serve to interpret phonemes or other linguistic units stand for these units, as the logician would

[13] E. Fischer-Jørgensen, 'Remarques sur les principes de l'analyse phonémique,' Travaux du Cercle Linguistique de Copenhague, V (1949), p. 231.

say. This difference has far-reaching consequences for the cardinally dissimilar patterning of letters and phonemes. Letters never, or only partially, reproduce the different distinctive features on which the phonemic pattern is based and unfailingly disregard the structural relationship of these features. There is no such thing in human society as the supplantation of the speech code by its visual replicas, but only a supplementation of this code by parasitic auxiliaries, while the speech code constantly and unalterably remains in effect. One could neither state that musical form is manifested in two variables – notes and sounds – nor that linguistic form is manifested in two equipollent substances – graphic and phonic. And just as musical form cannot be abstracted from the sound matter it organizes, so form in phonemics is to be studied in relation to the sound matter which the linguistic code selects, readjusts, dissects and classifies along its own lines. Like musical scales, phonemic patterning is an intervention of culture in nature, an artifact imposing logical rules upon the sound continuum.

2.5 *The cryptanalyst's and decoder's devices as two complementary techniques.* The addressee of a coded message is supposed to be in possession of the code and through it he interprets the message. Unlike this decoder, the cryptanalyst comes into possession of a message with no prior knowledge of the underlying code and must break this code through dexterous manipulations of the message. A native speaker responds to any text in his language as a regular decoder, whereas a stranger, unfamiliar with the language, faces the same text as a cryptanalyst. A linguist, approaching a totally unknown language, starts as a cryptanalyst until through a gradual breaking of its code he finally succeeds in approaching any message in this language like a native decoder.

The native or naturalized user of a language, when trained linguistically, is aware of the functions performed by its different sound elements and may utilize this knowledge to resolve the sound shape into its manifold information-bearing elements. He will employ various "grammatical pre-requisites to phonemic analysis" as aids to the extraction of destinctive, configurative and expressive features.[14]

On the other hand, the question raised by Bloch as to the applicability of the cryptanalyst's technique to the inquiry into phonemic structure has great methodological importance: to what extent might a sufficient sample of accurately recorded speech enable a linguist to work out "the phonemic system without knowing what any part of the sample meant, or even whether any two parts meant the same thing or different things".[15] Under such conditions, the extraction of redundant features is, in many instances, laborious but feasible. More difficult is the isolation of the expressive features but, in this regard also, the record may yield some information, given the difference between the markedly discrete, oppositional character of distinctive features and the more continuous "grading gamut" characterizing most of the expressive features.[16] Even a hybrid – bilingual or multilingual – message, as for instance, the sentences combined of Russian, French and English words or phrases, as used in the conversation of the Russian aristocracy in the late nineteenth century, could be, through the comparison of their heterogeneous phonetic make-up, roughly divided into monolingual sections: *"On se réunit le matin au breakfeast et puis vsjakij delaet čto xŏcet"* [õsə ʁeyní ləmat͡é obʁékfəst epu̯í fs,ákəj d, éləɪt ʃtɔxᵘóʃɪt], as Tolstoj reproduces the colloquial speech of his milieu in *Anna Karenina*.

An even less manageable problem would be the cryptanalytical discrimination between distinctive and configurative features, especially word border signals, e.g. it would hardly be possible to discover that in such Russian pairs of samples as /danós/ [danós] 'denunciation' – /da nós/ [dənós] 'and the nose too', /pagar,él,i/ [pəgar,él,i] '(they) burned up' – /pagar,é l,i/ [pəgar,él,i] 'whether along a mountain', /jixída/ [jix,ídə] 'spiteful person' – /jíx ída/

---

[14]   K. L. Pike, 'Grammatical prerequisites to phonemic analysis,' *Word*, III (1947), and 'More on grammatical prerequisites,' *Word*, VIII(1952).

[15]   B. Bloch, 'A set of postulates for phonemic analysis', *Language*, XXIV (1948).

[16]   Cf. Jakobson, Fant, Halle, *Preliminaries* ..., p. 15.

[jixídə] 'their Ida', the difference between [a] and the obscure [ə], the close [e] and the open [ę] or the palatalized [x,] and the non-palatalized [x] is not a distinction of two phonemes but only a word border signal. Here a cryptanalytical technique runs the risk of multiplying the number of Russian phonemes and distinctive features as compared to their actual stock.

THE IDENTIFICATION OF
DISTINCTIVE FEATURES

3.1 *Syllable.* The distinctive features are aligned into simultaneous bundles called phonemes; phonemes are concatenated into sequences; the elementary pattern underlying any grouping of phonemes is the syllable.[17] The phonemic structure of the syllable is determined by a set of rules and any sequence is based on the regular recurrence of this constructive model. A free form (a sequence, separable by means of pauses) must contain an integral number of syllables. Obviously, the number of different syllables in a language, is a small submultiple of the number of free forms, just as the number of phonemes is a small submultiple of the number of syllables, and the number of distinctive features, a submultiple of the number of phonemes.

The pivotal principle of syllable structure is the contrast of successive features within the syllable. One part of the syllable stands out from the others. It is mainly the contrast vowel *vs.* consonant which is used to render one part of the syllable more prominent. There are languages where every syllable consists of a consonant and a succeeding vowel (CV): in such a case it is possible from any point of the sequence to predict the class of phonemes that is to follow. In a language with a greater variety of syllable types, the recurrence of a phonemic class presents different degrees of probability. In addition to CV, other schemes may be used:

[17] E. Polivanov was the first to draw attention to the "phonemic syllable", he labelled *syllabeme*, as the basic constructive cell in the speech sequence: see his and A. Ivanov's *Grammatika sovremennogo kitaiskogo jazyka* (Moscow, 1930). Cf. A. Sommerfelt, 'Sur l'importance générale de la syllabe,' *Travaux du Cercle Linguistique de Prague*, IV (1931); A. W. de Groot, 'Voyelle, consonne et syllabe,' *Archives néerlandaises de phonétique expérimentale*, XVII (1941); J. Kuryłowicz, 'Contribution à la théorie de la syllabe,' *Bulletin de la Société Polonaise de Linguistique*, VIII (1948); J. D. O'Connor and J. L. M. Trim, 'Vowel, consonant, and syllable – a phonological definition,' *Word*, IX (1953).

CVC, V, VC. In contradistinction to C, the part V can neither be omitted, nor figure twice in the syllable.

The contrast vowel/consonant is either unique or merely predominant: it can be sporadically substituted by other cognate contrasts. Both part C and part V may contain more than one phoneme. The phonemes constituting parts V and C of the syllable are termed crest phonemes and slope phonemes respectively. If the crest contains two or more phonemes, one of them, termed the peak phoneme (or syllabic), is raised over the others by a contrast compact vs. diffuse or vowel vs. sonorant.

The motor correlate of the phonemic syllable has been most adequately described by Stetson[18] as "a puff of air forced upward through the vocal channel by a compression of the inter-costal muscles". According to this description, every syllable invariably consists of three successive factors: release, culmination, and arrest of the pulse. The middle one of these three phases is the nuclear factor of the syllable while the other two are marginal. Both marginal factors – initiation and termination – are effected either by the mere action of the chest muscles or by speech sounds, usually consonants. If both marginal factors are effected by the action of the chest muscles alone, the nuclear phase of the syllable is the only audible one; if, however, the release and/or the arrest is effected by speech sounds, the nuclear phase of the syllable is the most audible. In other words, the nuclear part of the syllable is in contrast to its marginal part as the crest to the slopes.

In the acoustic aspect, the crest usually exceeds the slopes in intensity and in many instances shows a higher fundamental frequency. Perceptually, the crest is distinguished from the slopes by a greater loudness, which is often accompanied by a heightened voice-pitch. As a rule, the crest phonemes are inherently louder than the slope phonemes of the same syllable: ordinarily the crest is formed by vowels, while the slopes contain the other phonemes; less frequently the contrast of crest and slope phonemes is displayed

[18]   R. H. Stetson, *Motor phonetics* (Amsterdam, 1951).

by liquids *vs.* pure consonants; or by nasals *vs.* oral consonants, and
in exceptional cases by constrictives *vs.* stops (cf. 4.16). If a
slope is constituted by a whole cluster and if within such a cluster
there is an inherently louder phoneme in less loud surroundings, its
loudness is noticeably reduced to preserve the unity of the syllable:
e.g. Czech /jdu/, /jsem/, /rti/, /lpi/, or Polish monosyllable /krvi/ *vs.*
Serbocroatian disyllabic /krvi/.[19]

3.2 *Two kinds of distinctive features.* The distinctive features are
divided into two classes: 1) p r o s o d i c and 2) i n h e r e n t. A
prosodic feature is displayed only by those phonemes which form
the crest of the syllable and it may be defined only with reference
to the relief of the syllable or of the syllable chain, whereas the
inherent feature is displayed by phonemes irrespective of their role
in the relief of the syllable, and the definition of such a feature does
not refer to the relief of the syllable or of the syllable chain.

3.3 *Classification of prosodic features.* The three types of prosodic
features, which, following Sweet, we term t o n e, f o r c e, and
q u a n t i t y, correspond to the three attributes of sensation – voice-
pitch, voice-loudness and subjective duration. The dimensions of
frequency, intensity and time are their closest physical correlates.
Each of these three sub-classes of prosodic features presents two
varieties: according to its frame of reference a prosodic feature may
be either i n t e r s y l l a b i c or i n t r a s y l l a b i c. In the first case, the
crest of one syllable is compared with the crests of other syllables
within the same sequence. In the second case, an instant pertaining
to the crest may be compared with other instants of the same crest
or with the subsequent slope.

3.31 *Tone features.* In the intersyllabic variety of tone features –
the l e v e l feature, different syllable crests within a sequence are
contrasted by their register: higher and lower. The level feature
may be split in two: either a neutral register is contrasted with an

[19]   See particularly A. Ābele, 'K voprosu o sloge,' *Slavia*, III (1924).

elevated register, on the one hand, and with a lowered one, on the other, or, finally, each of the two opposite registers, high and low, may appear in two varieties, raised and diminished. When the Jabo people transpose these four levels from speech into drum signals, they use for the two underlying oppositions two different pairs of terms: the opposites high and low are called "little bird" and "big bird", while the opposites raised and diminished are termed "smaller" and "larger", so that the four signals are distinguished – "smaller little bird", "larger little bird", "smaller big bird", and "larger big bird".[20] The voice-tone mechanism has been closely investigated by Farnsworth, who states that the motion of the vocal cords, more complex at low frequencies of vibration, becomes simplified as the rate is raised, until at the highest frequencies of vibration, only the edges of the cords nearest the glottis are seen to vibrate.[21]

The intrasyllabic variety of tone features, the modulation feature, contrasts the higher register of one portion of a phoneme with a lower register of another portion of the same phoneme, or the higher register of one component of a diphthong with the lower register of its other components, and this distribution of registers within the crests of the syllable is opposed to the reverse distribution, e.g. a rising modulation to a falling one, or both of them to an even intonation.

3.32 *Force features.* The intersyllabic variety of the force features, the s t r e s s feature, is a contrast of a louder, stressed crest to the less loud, unstressed crests of other syllables within the same sequence, a difference produced by the sublaryngeal mechanism, in particular by the abdomen-diaphragmal movements, as Sievers and Stetson attempt to prove.[22]

[20] See G. Herzog, 'Drum signaling in West African tribes,' *Word*, I (1945).
[21] D. W. Farnsworth, 'High-speed motion picture of the human vocal cords,' *Bell Laboratories Record*, V (1940).
[22] E. Sievers, 'Neues zu den Rutzschen Reaktionen,' *Archiv für experimentelle und klinische Phonetik*, I (1914); R. H. Stetson, *l.c.* Cf. W. F. Twaddell, 'Stetsons's model and the "supra-segmental phonemes",' *Language*, XXIX (1953).

In the intrasyllabic variety of the stress features, the so-called
stosston (stød) feature, two contiguous fractions of the stressed
phoneme are compared with each other. To an even distribution
of loudness throughout the phoneme, another type is opposed:
the initial portion of the phoneme presents the peak of loudness,
whereas in the final portion the loudness decreases. According
to S. Smith's analysis of the Danish stød,[23] the decline of amplitude,
often accompanied by a decrease of the fundamental frequency,
is due to an abruptly decreasing innervation of the expiratory
muscles. A ballistic movement of the expiratory muscles, opposed
to a more even movement, produces a similar prosodic feature,
e.g., in Latvian, Lithuanian dialects and Livian.

3.33 *Quantity features.* The intersyllabic variety of quantity
features, the length feature, contrasts a normal, short, unstretch-
able phoneme within the crest of the syllable with the long,
sustained phonemes of the other syllables in the same sequence,
and/or a normal, short but steady phoneme with a punctual,
reduced, transient one.

The second variety of the quantity features, the contact
feature, is based on a different distribution of duration between
the vowel and the subsequent consonant: in the case of the so-
called close contact (*scharf geschnittener Akzent*), the vowel is
abridged in favor of the following, arresting consonant, whereas
at the open contact (*schwach geschnittener Akzent*), the vowel
displays its full extent before the consonant starts.

3.34 *The interconnection between stress and length.* Wherever
there is a contrast of stressed and unstressed syllables, stress is
always used as a configurative, namely culminative feature, whereas
length never assumes this function. The culminative function of
the stress is regularly combined either with the other variety of
configurative functions, the demarcation (cf. 2.3), or with the
distinctive function. Languages where both length and stress
appear as distinctive features are quite exceptional, and if the stress

---

[23] S. Smith, 'Contributions to the solution of problems concerning the
Danish stød,' *Nordisk Tidsskrift for Tale og Stemme*, VIII (1944).

is distinctive the latter is mostly supplemented by a redundant length.

The observation of force and quantity features in their inter-syllabic variety seems to indicate that the prosodic distinctive features utilizing intensity and those utilizing time tend to merge.

3.4 *Comparison of prosodic and inherent features.* Any prosodic feature is based primarily on the contrast between two variables within one and the same time sequence: the relative voice-pitch, voice-loudness or duration of a given fraction is determined with respect to preceding and/or succeeding fractions. As Herzog has pointed out concerning the tone features, "the actualizations of the contrasts – given by successive distances between tone levels or by successive tone movements – do shift all the time."[24] Tone level, or tone modulation, stress degrees or its decrescendo (*stosston*), are always purely relative and highly variable in their absolute magnitudes from speaker to speaker, and even from one utterance to another in the usage of the same speaker. Also the quantity of a vowel may be established only in relation to the quantity of the other vowels within the context or to the subsequent consonants (contact feature), while the absolute duration of the long or short vowels in the given language presents a considerable vacillation in speed, depending upon the speech-habits of the speaker and his expressive variations of tempo. A long vowel must be *ceteris paribus* longer than the surrounding short vowels. Similarly, the only thing required of a stressed vowel is to be uttered in a louder voice than the unstressed vowels of the same chain; and the high register vowels must be of a higher voice-tone than the neighboring low register vowels. But the high register vowels of one, e.g. bass speaker, may be even deeper than the low register vowels of another, e.g. soprano speaker, and in the speech of one and the same person there may be passages with relative expressive lowering of both high and low register phonemes.

A prosodic feature involves two coordinates: on the one hand,

[24] G. Herzog, review of K. L. Pike, *Tone languages*, in *International Journal of American Linguistics*, XV (1949).

polar terms such as high and low register, rising and falling pitch, or long and short, all may appear, *ceteris paribus*, in the same position in the sequence, so that the speaker selectively uses and the listener selectively apprehends one of the two alternatives and identifies the chosen alternative in relation to the rejected one. These two alternatives, the one present and the other absent in the given unit of the message, constitute a veritable logical opposition (cf. 1.3). On the other hand, both polar terms are fully recognizable only when both of them are present in the given sequence, so that the speaker effects and the listener perceives their contrast. Thus both alternatives of a prosodic feature coexist in the code as two terms of an opposition and, moreover, co-occur and produce a contrast within the message. If the message is too brief to include both contrasting units, the feature may be inferred from the substitutive clues offered by the sequence, e.g. the quantity of a vowel in a monosyllable message may be inferred from the relative duration of the surrounding consonants, and the register of a monophonemic message, from the modulation span in the onset and/or decay of the vowel.

The recognition and definition of an inherent feature is based only on the choice between two alternatives admissible in the same position within a sequence. No comparison of the two polar terms co-occurring within one context is involved. Hence, both alternatives of an inherent feature co-exist in the code as two terms of an opposition, but do not require a contrasting juxtaposition within one message. Since the inherent feature is identified only through the comparison of the alternative present in the given position with the absent alternative, the implementation of an inherent feature in a given position admits less variability than that of the prosodic features.

3.5 *General laws of phonemic patterning.* The comparative description of the phonemic systems of diverse languages and their confrontation with the order of phonemic acquisitions by infants learning to speak, as well as with the gradual dismantling of language and of its phonemic pattern in aphasia, gives us important insights into the interrelation and classification of the distinctive features. The linguistic, especially phonemic progress of the child and the regression of the aphasic obey the same laws of implication. If the child's acquisition of distinction B implies his acquisition of distinction A, the loss of A in aphasia implies the absence of B, and the rehabilitation of the aphasic follows the same order as the child's phonemic development. The same laws of implication underlie the languages of the world both in their static and dynamic aspects. The presence of B implies the presence of A and, correspondingly, B cannot emerge in the phonemic pattern of a language unless A is there; likewise, A cannot disappear from a language as long as B exists. The more limited the number of languages possessing a certain phonemic feature or combination of features, the later is it acquired by the native children and the earlier is it lost by the native aphasics.

3.51 *Restrictions in the over-all inventory of distinctive features.* The progressing phonemic investigation of infants and aphasics,[25] along with the ever increasing number of detected laws, moves into the foreground the problem of the universal rules underlying the phonemic patterning of languages. In view of these laws of implication and stratification, the phonemic typology of languages is becoming an ever more feasible and urgent task. Every step in this direction permits us to reduce the list of distinctive features used in the languages of the world. The supposed multiplicity of features proves to be largely illusory. If two or more allegedly different features never co-occur in a language and if they,

[25] Cf. R. Jakobson, 'Kindersprache, Aphasie und allgemeine Lautgesetze,' *Uppsala Universitets Årsskrift* (1942); H. V. Velten, 'The growth of phonemic and lexical patterns in infant language,' *Language*, XIX (1943); W. F. Leopold, *Speech development of a bilingual child*, II (Evanston, 1947); A. Gvozdev, *Usvoenie rebenkom zvukovoj storony russkogo jazyka* (Moscow, 1948); K. Ohnesorg, *Fonetická studie o dětské řeči* (Prague, 1948); L. Kaczmarek, *Ksztaltowanie się mowy dziecka* (Poznan, 1953); P. Smoczyński, *Przyswajanie przez dziecko podstaw systemu językowego* (Lodz, 1955). – Th. Alajouanine, A. Ombredane, M. Durand, *Le syndrome de désintégration phonétique dans l'aphasie* (Paris, 1939); A. Luria, *Travmatičeskaja afazija* (Moscow, 1947); K. Goldstein, *Language and language disturbances* (New York, 1948).

furthermore, yield a common property distinguishing them from all other features, then they are to be interpreted as different implementations of one and the same feature, each occurring to the exclusion of the others and, consequently, presenting a particular case of complementary distribution. The study of invariances within the phonemic pattern of one language must be supplemented by a search for universal invariances in the phonemic patterning of language.

Thus no language simultaneously displays two autonomous consonantal oppositions – pharyngealized/non-pharyngealized and rounded/unrounded. The back orifice of the mouth resonator (pharynx) is involved in the first instance and the front orifice (lips) in the second, but in both cases a narrowed orifice of the mouth resonator, producing a downward shift in the resonances, is opposed to the absence of narrowing. Hence these two processes (narrowed back slit and narrowed front slit) are to be treated as two variants of one and the same opposition which on the motor level may be defined as narrowed *vs.* adjusted slit (cf. 3.62). The relation of retroflex to the dental consonants proves to be a mere variety of the opposition of pharyngealized and non-pharyngealized dentals.

Four consonantal features listed by Trubetzkoy (*l.c.*, pp. 132f.) – the tension feature, the intensity or pressure feature, the aspiration feature and the pre-aspiration feature – also turn out to be complementary variants of one and the same opposition which by virtue of its common denominator may be termed tense/lax.

Double stops (particularly clicks) with closures in rapid succession, followed by two distinct releases in the same order, appear to the exclusion of other types of clusters in the same positions and present simply a different implementation of ordinary consonantal sequences.[26]

3.6 *The two classes of inherent features.* The inherent distinctive features which have so far been discovered in the languages of the world and which, along with the prosodic features, underlie their

[26]   Cf. C. M. Doke, 'Notes on a problem in the mechanism of the Zulu clicks,' *Bantu Studies*, II (1923).

entire lexical and morphological stock, amount to twelve oppositions, out of which each language makes its own selection. All
the inherent features are divided into two classes that might
be termed s o n o r i t y f e a t u r e s and t o n a l i t y f e a t u r e s, the
former akin to the prosodic force and quantity features and the
latter to the prosodic pitch features. The sonority features utilize
the amount and concentration of energy in the spectrum and in
time. The tonality features involve the ends of the frequency
spectrum.

3.61   *Sonority features*

I. V o c a l i c / n o n - v o c a l i c :

acoustically – presence *vs.* absence of a sharply defined formant
structure;
genetically – primary or only excitation at the glottis together
with a free passage through the vocal tract.

II. C o n s o n a n t a l / n o n - c o n s o n a n t a l :

acoustically – low (*vs.* high) total energy;
genetically – presence *vs.* absence of an obstruction in the vocal
tract.

   V o w e l s are vocalic and non-çonsonantal; c o n s o n a n t s are
consonantal and non-vocalic; l i q u i d s are vocalic and consonantal
(with both free passage and obstruction in the oral cavity and the
córresponding acoustic effect); g l i d e s are non-vocalic and non-
consonantal.

III. C o m p a c t / d i f f u s e :

acoustically – higher (*vs.* lower) concentration of energy in a
relatively narrow, central region of the spectrum, accompanied
by an increase (*vs.* decrease) of the total amount of energy;
genetically – forward-flanged *vs.* backward-flanged. The difference
lies in the relation between the volume of the resonance chamber
in front of the narrowest stricture and behind this stricture.
The ratio of the former to the latter is higher for the forward-
flanged phonemes (wide vowels, and velar and palatal, including

post-alveolar, consonants) than for the corresponding backward-flanged phonemes (narrow vowels, and labial and dental, including alveolar, consonants).

IV. Tense/lax:

acoustically – higher (*vs.* lower) total amount of energy in conjunction with a greater (*vs.* smaller) spread of the energy in the spectrum and in time;

genetically – greater (*vs.* smaller) deformation of the vocal tract – away from its rest position. The role of muscular strain affecting the tongue, the walls of the vocal tract and the glottis requires further examination.

V. Voiced/voiceless:

acoustically – presence *vs.* absence of periodic low frequency excitation;

genetically – periodic vibrations of the vocal cords *vs.* lack of such vibrations.

VI. Nasal/oral (nasalized/non-nasalized):

acoustically – spreading the available energy over wider (*vs.* narrower) frequency regions by a reduction in the intensity of certain (primarily the first) formants and introduction of additional (nasal) formants;

genetically – mouth resonator supplemented by the nose cavity *vs.* the exclusion of the nasal resonator.

VII. Discontinuous/continuant:

acoustically – silence (at least in frequency range above vocal cord vibration) followed and/or preceded by spread of energy over a wide frequency region (either as burst or as a rapid transition of vowel formants) *vs.* absence of abrupt transition between sound and such a silence;

genetically – rapid turning on or off of source either through a rapid closure and/or opening of the vocal tract that distinguishes plosives from constrictives or through one or more taps that differentiate the discontinuous liquids like a flap or trill /r/ from continuant liquids like the lateral /l/.

VIII. Strident/mellow:

acoustically – higher intensity noise *vs.* lower intensity noise;
genetically – rough-edged *vs.* smooth-edged: supplementary obstruction creating edge effects (*Schneidenton*) at the point of articulation distinguishes the production of the rough-edged phonemes
from the less complex impediment in their smooth-edged counter-
parts.

IX. Checked/unchecked:

acoustically – higher rate of discharge of energy within a reduced
interval of time *vs.* lower rate of discharge within a longer interval;
genetically – glottalized (with compression or closure of the glottis)
vs. non-glottalized.

3.62   *Tonality features.*

X. Grave/acute:

acoustically – concentration of energy in the lower (*vs.* upper)
frequencies of the spectrum;
genetically – peripheral *vs.* medial: peripheral phonemes (velar and
labial) have an ampler and less compartmented resonator than the
corresponding medial phonemes (palatal and dental).

XI. Flat/plain:

acoustically – flat phonemes in contradistinction to the corresponding plain ones are characterized by a downward shift or
weakening of some of their upper frequency components;
genetically – the former (narrowed slit) phonemes in contradistinction to the latter (wider slit) phonemes are produced with a
decreased back or front orifice of the mouth resonator, and a
concomitant velarization expanding the mouth resonator.

XII. Sharp/plain:

acoustically – sharp phonemes in contradistinction to the corresponding plain ones are characterized by an upward shift of some
of their upper frequency components;
genetically – the sharp (widened slit) *vs.* plain (narrower slit)
phonemes exhibit a dilated pharyngeal pass, i.e. a widened back

orifice of the mouth resonator; a concomitant palatalization restricts and compartments the mouth cavity.

3.7 *Stages of the speech event.* Each of the distinctive features has been defined above both on its acoustical and articulatory level. The communication network, however, comprises a higher number of stages. The initial stage in any speech event – the intention of the sender – is not yet open to a precise analysis. The same may be said of the nerve impulses sent from the brain to the effector organs. The work of these organs – the motor stage of the speech event – is at present quite accessible to observation, especially with the progress of X-rays and other tools that uncover the activities of such highly important parts of the speech apparatus as the pharyngeal, laryngeal and sub-laryngeal mechanisms. The status of the message between the bodily pathways of the speaker and listener, the transmitted vibrations in the air, are ever more adequately mastered, owing especially to the amazing advance of modern acoustics.

The translation of the physical stimulus, first into aural and then into neural processes, is about to be charted.[27] The search for the models of distinctive features used by the auditory system is a timely task. As to the transformation of speech components by the nervous system, we can, for the time being, at best only hazard what psychophysiologists have intimated as "a mere speculative assertion":[28] sonority features seem to be related to the amount, density and spread of nervous excitation, while the tonality features relate to the location of this excitation. The present development of research on the neural responses to sound stimuli promises, however, to supply a differential picture of distinctive features on this level as well.

The psychological study of sound perception has endeavored

---

[27] For tentative moves in this direction, see J. C. R. Licklider, 'On the process of speech perception,' *Journal of the Acoustical Society of America,* XXIV (1952); H. Mol and E. M. Uhlenbeck, 'The analysis of the phoneme in distinctive features and the process of hearing,' *Lingua,* IV (1954).

[28] S. S. Stevens and H. Davis, *Hearing* (New York, 1938), p. 164.

to isolate the diverse subjective attributes of sound and to determine the discriminatory capacity of the listeners for each of the dimensions of the stimulus. The expansion of this investigation to speech sounds is likely to illuminate the perceptual correlates of the diverse distinctive features in view of their phenomenal autonomy. The initial experiments on English consonants transmitted with frequency distortion and with random masking noise have actually confirmed that the perception of each of these features is relatively independent of the perception of the others, as if "separate, simple channels were involved rather than a single complex channel."[29]

To a psychologist, each attribute is defined through a differential reaction to a stimulus by a listener under a particular s e t (*Aufgabe*). In application to speech sounds this set is determined by the decoding attitude of the listener to the message received and to each of its constituents. The listener correlates the incoming message with the code common to himself and the speaker. Thus the role of sound components and combinations in the linguistic pattern is implicit in the perception of speech sounds. To find out what motor, acoustic and perceptual elements of sounds are utilized in a given language, we must be guided by its coding rules: an efficacious physiological, physical and psychological analysis of speech sounds presupposes their linguistic interpretation.

3.71 *The use of different stages in the study of distinctive features.* In order to decode the message, its receiver extracts the distinctive features from the perceptual data. The closer we are in our investigation to the destination of the message, the more accurately

---

[29]   G. A. Miller and P. E. Nicely, 'An analysis of perceptual confusions among some English consonants,' *Journal of the Acoustical Society of America*, XXVII (1955). A fruitful check of the distinctive features on the perceptual level may also be expected from the experiments in progress at the Haskins Laboratories (New York) on the perception of synthetic speech sounds. Furthermore, a cautious study of synesthetic associations between phonemic features and color attributes should yield clues to the perceptual aspect of speech sounds. There seems to be a phenomenal affinity between optimal chromaticity (pure red) and vocalic compactness, attenuated chromaticity (yellow—blue) and vocalic diffuseness, optimal achromaticity (black—white) and consonantal diffuseness, attentuated achromaticity (grayed) and consonantal compactness; moreover between the value axis of colors (dark—light) and the tonality axis in language,

can we gauge the information conveyed by the sound-chain. This determines the operational hierarchy of levels in their decreasing pertinence: perceptual, aural, acoustical and motor (the latter carrying no direct information to the receiver except for the sporadic help of lip-reading). The auditory experience is the only aspect of the encoded message actually shared by the sender and the receiver since the speaker normally hears himself.

In the process of communication there is no single-valued inference from a succeeding to a preceding stage. With each successive stage, the selectivity increases; some data of an antecedent stage are irrelevant for any subsequent stage, and each item of the latter stage may be a function of several variables from the former stage. The measurement of the vocal tract permits an exact prediction of the sound wave, but one and the same acoustical effect may be attained by altogether different means. Similarly, the same attribute of the auditory sensation may be the result of different physical stimuli.

The theoretically unlikely surmise of a closer relationship between perception and articulation than between perception and its immediate stimulus finds no corroboration in experience: the kinaesthetic feedback of the listener plays a very subordinate and incidental role. Not seldom do we acquire the ability to discern foreign phonemes by ear without having mastered their production, and in a child's learning of language an auditory discrimination of adults' phonemes often precedes the use of these phonemes in his own speech.

The specification of distinctive oppositions may be made with respect to any stage of the speech event, from articulation to perception and decoding, on the sole condition that the invariants of any antecedent stage be selected and correlated in terms of the subsequent stages, given the evident fact that we speak to be heard and need to be heard in order to be understood.

The distinctive features have been portrayed only on the motor and on the acoustic level, because these are the only two aspects for which we so far possess detailed information. Either of these two patterns must give the complete picture of all the ultimate, further irreducible distinctions. But since articulation is to acoustic phenomenon as means to effect, the classification of motor data must be made with reference to the acoustic patterns. Thus, the difference among four articulatory classes of consonants – velar, palatal, dental and labial – dissolves itself on the acoustic level into two binary oppositions: on the one hand, labials and velars coneentrate their energy in the lower frequencies of the spectrum in contradistinction to dentals and palatals, which concentrate their energy in the upper frequencies – the grave/acute opposition. On the other hand, velars and palatals are distinguished from labials and dentals by a greater concentration of energy – the compact/diffuse opposition. The gravity of the labials and velars is generated by a larger and less divided mouth cavity, and the acuteness of dentals and palatals, by a smaller and more compartmented cavity. Thus, on the motor level, the decisive difference is between the stricture in a medial region of the mouth – dental or palatal – and a stricture in a peripheral region – labial or velar. An identical articulatory difference opposes the velar to palatal vowels (back – front) as acoustically grave *vs*. acute. A larger volume of the resonating cavity in front of the point of articulation and a smaller volume of the cavity behind this point distinguishes velar from labial consonants and palatal from dental consonants and engenders the compactness of velars and palatals. The same articulatory factor determines the compactness of the wide vowels *vs*. the diffuseness of the narrow vowels. It would have been much more difficult to extract the common denominator of the distinctions between labial and dental consonants and velar and palatal consonants or vowels, as well as the common denominator of the distinctions between velars and labials, palatals and dentals, wide and narrow vowels, if the striking acoustical and perceptual oppositions grave/acute and compact/diffuse were not taken into account.

Although it was evident to observers that among plosives, the labio-dental, alveolar (hissing), post-alveolar (hushing) and uvular affricates are opposed by their noisy friction to the bilabial, dental, palatal and velar stops, nonetheless a similar opposition between

the corresponding constrictives was usually overlooked, notwithstanding that all these affricates and the homorganic constrictives
are distinguished by a special kind of turbulence due to forcing the
air stream over a supplementary barrier (the edge of the teeth or
uvula). In the spectrogram, the random distribution of black areas
in these strident consonants, as compared with the considerably
more regular patterns in the mellow consonants, is the only
differentiating clue for all such pairs, and this clue, common to all
the pairs in question, reveals a distinct binary opposition.

3.72 *Nomenclature of distinctive features.* Traditional terminology
resorted indiscriminately to different stages of the speech event:
terms such as nasal, palatalized, rounded, glottalized, referred to
the motor level; other labels (voiced, high, falling, pitch, lenis,
liquid) referred partly to the acoustical, partly to the perceptual
aspect, and even when a figurative term was used, it had some basis
in phenomenal experience. Insofar as the feature we define has a
traditional term, we use the latter regardless of the stage of the
speech event to which it relates, e.g. nasal/oral, tense/lax, voiced/
voiceless, stressed/unstressed. A traditional articulatory term is
retained as long as it points to an important criterion of division
with respect to the sound transmitted, perceived and decoded. In
several cases, however, there is no current phonetic term to cover
the feature we define. For such features we take over terms from
acoustics or psycho-acoustics. But since each of these features is
definable and has actually been defined both on the acoustic and
on the motor level, any of them could with equal right bear a
newly-coined articulatory designation such as forward-flanged/
backward-flanged instead of compact/diffuse, rough-edged/
smooth-edged instead of strident/mellow, peripheral/medial
instead of grave/acute, narrowed slit/wider slit instead of
flat/plain and widenend slit/narrower slit instead of
sharp/plain.

 We are not concerned with substituting an acoustic classification
for an articulatory one but solely in uncovering the most productive
criteria of division valid for both aspects.

PHONEMIC PATTERNING

4.1 *Stratification: nuclear syllable.* Ordinarily child language begins, and the aphasic dissolution of language preceding its complete loss ends, with what psychopathologists have termed the "labial stage". In this phase speakers are capable only of one type of utterance, which is usually transcribed as /pa/. From the articulatory point of view the two constituents of this utterance represent polar configurations of the vocal tract: in /p/ the tract is closed at its very end while in /a/ it is opened as widely as possible at the front and narrowed toward the back, thus assuming the horn-shape of a megaphone. This combination of two extremes is also apparent on the acoustic level: the labial stop presents a momentary burst of sound without any great concentration of energy in a particular frequency band, whereas in the vowel /a/ there is no strict limitation of time, and the energy is concentrated in a relatively narrow region of maximum aural sensitivity. In the first constituent there is an extreme limitation in the time domain but no ostensible limitation in the frequency domain, whereas the second constituent shows no ostensible limitation in the time domain but a maximum limitation in the frequency domain. Consequently, the diffuse stop with its maximal reduction in the energy output offers the closest approach to silence, while the open vowel represents the highest energy output of which the human vocal apparatus is capable.

This polarity between the minimum and the maximum of energy appears primarily as a contrast between two successive units – the optimal consonant and the optimal vowel. Thus the elementary phonemic frame, the syllable, is established. Since many languages lack syllables without a prevocalic consonant and/or with a post-vocalic consonant, CV (Consonant + Vowel) is the only universal model of the syllable.

4.12 *The role of the nasal consonant.* The choice between /pa/ and /a/ and/or /pa/ and /ap/ may become the first carrier of meaning in the very early stages of child language. Usually, however, the infant preserves for a time a constant syllable scheme and splits both constituents of this syllable, first the consonant and later the vowel, into distinctive alternatives.

Most frequently, the oral stop, utilizing a single closed tract, obtains a counterpart in the nasal consonant, which combines a closed main tract with an open subsidiary tract and thereby supplements the specific traits of a stop with a secondary vocalic characteristic. Before there appeared the consonantal opposition nasal/oral, consonant was distinguished from vowel as closed tract from open tract. Once the nasal consonant is opposed to the oral as presence to absence of the open tract, the contrast consonant/vowel is revalued as presence *vs.* absence of a closed tract.

Various further oppositions, modifying and attenuating the primary optimal contrast of consonant and vowel follow. All these later formations reshape in some way the mouth resonator, while nasalization merely adds a secondary resonating cavity to the mouth resonator without changing its volume and shape.

The opposition of nasal and oral consonant, which belongs to the earliest acquisitions of the child, is ordinarily the most resistant consonantal opposition in aphasia and it occurs in all the languages of the world except for some American Indian languages.

4.13 *The primary triangle.* The opposition nasal *vs.* oral stop, however, may be preceded by the split of the stop into two opposites, labial and dental. After the appearance of the contrast CV, founded upon one attribute of sound, loudness, the utilization of the other basic attribute, pitch, is psychologically inferable. Thus the first tonality opposition is instituted: grave/acute, in other words, the concentration of energy in the lower *vs.* upper frequencies of the spectrum. In /p/ the lower end predominates, while in /t/ the upper end is the stronger one. It is quite natural that the first tonality feature should affect not the vowel /a/, with its maximal concentration of energy in a narrow central region of the spectrum, but the consonant /p/, with its maximal diffusion of energy over a wide frequency band.

At this stage the pole of high and concentrated energy /a/ contrasts with the low energy stops /p/ and /t/. Both stops are opposed to each other by a predominance of one or the other end of the frequency spectrum, as the gravity and acuteness poles. These two dimensions underlie a t r i a n g u l a r pattern of phonemes (or at least of oral phonemes if the nasality feature has already emerged):

4.14 *The split of the primary triangle into two triangles, consonantal and vocalic.* The rise of the consonantal tonality feature is followed by the first vocalic split. The polarity of two successive units, CV, based on the contrast of reduced and full energy is supplemented by a polarity of two alternative vowels, founded on the opposition of lower and higher concentration of energy. The single compact /a/ finds its opposite in a diffuse vowel. Henceforth, both the consonantal and the vocalic section of the primary triangle construct each its own linear pattern – the grave/acute consonantal axis and the compact/diffuse vocalic axis.

The consonants duplicate this originally vocalic opposition and the consonantal base-line of the over-all triangle proves to be complemented by a consonantal apex – the velar stop that Grimm had already justly defined as the "fullest of all producible consonants".

The tonality opposition, originally consonantal, may in turn be extended to the vocalic pattern: it is naturally the diffuse vowel that splits into grave and acute, complementing the vocalic apex of the over-all triangle by a /u/ – /i/ base-line. In this way the originally single primary triangle is split into two autonomous two-dimensional patterns – the consonantal and the vocalic triangle.

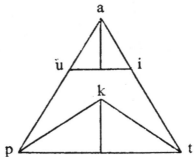

4.15 *Patterning of oral resonance features.* Both the vocalic and the consonantal pattern may subsequently pass from the triangular to the quadrangular pattern by superimposing the distinction between velar and palatal upon the wide vowels and/or upon the consonants. In this way the grave/acute feature spreads to the compact vowels and/or consonants. In the languages of the world, however, the triangular pattern prevails over the quadrangular for vowels and even more so for consonants – it is the minimum model, both for the vocalic and for the consonantal patterns, with the very rare exceptions when either the vocalic or the consonantal pattern – but never both – is linear. In the rare cases of a linear patterning, the vowels are confined to the feature compact/diffuse and the consonants, almost unfailingly, to the tonality feature. Thus no language lacks the oppositions grave/acute and compact/diffuse, whereas any other opposition may be absent.

The alternation in volume and shape of the mouth resonator is used for the grave/acute opposition. In the early stages of child language, in the advanced stages of aphasia and in numerous languages of the world, this alternation is reinforced by the variation in the size of one or both orifices of the mouth cavity. The restriction of the back and front orifices, together with an expanded and unified oral cavity, serve to lower the resonance frequencies, whereas the combined action of the dilated orifices and of a restricted and compartmented cavity raise the resonance frequencies. But the change in the size of each of these orifices may achieve an autonomous status and set in operation secondary tonality features (flatting and/or sharping).

The development of the oral resonance features in child language presents a whole chain of successive acquisitions interlinked by laws of implication. We tentatively tabulate this temporal series in the following chart, using for the distinctions acquired the traditional articulatory terms and designating each of these acquisitions by a sequence of numbers preceded by 0., i.e. writing each sequence as a decimal fraction. The sequences were composed in such a way that if sequence S_1 is assigned to distinction A and sequence S_2 to distinction B, and S_1 is an initial subsequence of S_2 (i.e. S_1 is an initial subsequence of S_2 if the first digits of S_2 are identical with S_1; e.g. $S_1 = 0.19$ and $S_2 = 0.195$), then the acquisition of distinction B implies that of A. The numerical values of the digits and their number have no other significance. It is obvious that only those distinctions are acquired by the child that are present in the language being learned.

Consonants: dental vs. labial 0.1
Vowels: narrow vs. wide 0.11
Narrow vowels: palatal vs. velar 0.111
Wide vowels: palatal vs. velar 0.1111
Narrow palatal vowels: rounded vs. unrounded . . 0.1112
Wide palatal vowels: rounded vs. unrounded . . 0.11121
Velar vowels: unrounded vs. rounded 0.1113
Consonants: velopalatal vs. labial and dental . . . 0.112
Consonants: palatal vs. velar 0.1121
Consonants: rounded vs. unrounded or
        pharyngealized vs. non-pharyngealized . 0.1122
Consonants: palatalized vs. non-palatalized . . . 0.1123

4.16 *Sonority features in relation to the optimal consonant and vowel.* The reduced concentration of energy in the diffuse vowel moves it away from the optimal, compact vowel in the direction of the consonants and, conversely, the reduced spread of energy in the compact consonant diverts it from the optimal, diffuse consonant in the direction of the vowel.

In the nasal consonants the addition of the new, open resonator superimposes sharply-defined nasal formants upon the spectrum of the oral stop. Nasal resonance brings consonants closer to vowels and, on the other hand, when superimposed upon a vocalic spectrum, damps the other formants and deflects the vowel from its optimal pattern.

The optimal, stop consonant finds its opposite in the constrictive that attenuates the consonantal reduction of energy. Stops are an earlier acquisition of children and a later loss of aphasics than constrictive phonemes. There are in the world several languages without constrictives but no languages without stops.

The appearance of liquids which combine the clear-cut formant structure of a vowel with the consonantal reduction of energy, changes the contrast consonant/vowel into two autonomous oppositions, consonantal/non-consonantal and vocalic/non-vocalic. While the consonantal feature, reduction of energy, is optimally represented by the stop, which tends toward a single pulse, the non-vocalic feature, absence of sharply-defined formant structure, is optimally manifested by the strident consonant which tends toward white noise. Therefore, the emancipation of the two features from each other, discontinuous/continuant on the one hand, and strident/ mellow on the other, implies the acquisition of a liquid that combines two autonomous features, the vocalic and the consonantal. Actually, mellow constrictives, opposed to strident constrictives, or strident plosives (affricates) opposed to mellow plosives (stops proper) do not appear in child language before the emergence of the first liquid, and under aphasia, vanish when the liquids are lost.

Strident plosives, in contradistinction to mellow plosives, attenuate the consonantal reduction of energy. The mellow constrictives deviate from the non-vocalic optimum embodied in the strident constrictives, namely from their markedly noisy pattern. One and the same split of the consonantal feature, on the one hand, and of the non-vocalic feature, on the other, is manifested both in the appearance of the liquids and of the strident stops. This explains the "strange but widespread" interchangeability of strident stops and liquids, especially laterals, that Bouda notes in Manchu-Tungus and in Paleosiberian languages.[30]

Since nasality, by superimposing a clear-cut formant structure upon the consonantal pattern, brings consonants closer to vowels, and since liquids combine the consonantal with the vocalic feature, it is advantageous to range these two related classes of phonemes under a common heading of s o n o r a n t s. The consonantal character of these two classes is again reinforced in such relatively rare phonemes as the discontinuous nasals (the so-called prenasalized stops) and the strident liquids (the sibilant laterals or vibrant).

The oral phonemes with an obstructed vocal tract have a noise source at the obstruction and may use voice – if ever – only as a supplementary source, whereas for the phonemes with an open tract, the voice is the main source. While the optimal consonant is voiceless and the optimal vowel voiced, the voicing of consonants or, in very rare instances the unvoicing of vowels, may be utilized as one of the various attenuations of the maximum contrast CV.

Since the consonant is primarily characterized by reduction of energy, the optimal consonant is lax but may be subsequently opposed by a tense consonant that attenuates the contrast between consonant and vowel. Normally, however, the voiced consonant is of lower energy than the voiceless and therefore, in the opposition of tense and lax consonants, the laxness is frequently accompanied by voicing and the tenseness by voicelessness, so that the consonant, optimal in one respect – reduction of energy – deviates from the consonantal optimum in another way, the presence of voice. If both oppositions act autonomously in a language, the doubly optimal consonant, lax and voiceless, is opposed by two phonemes, one, a voiceless tense and the other, a voiced lax, both of which, in different ways, shift the structure of the consonant toward that of the vowel. A further move in this direction is a consonant

[30] K. Bouda, 'Lateral und Sibilant,' *Zeitschrift für Phonetik*, I (1947).

endowed with the distinctive features of tenseness and voicing, such as /dᶜ/ in some languages of India.

Normally, the total energy of a vowel increases along with concentration of energy (compactness), but in a tense vowel, as compared with the corresponding lax vowel, the total energy increases, whereas the concentration of energy decreases. This reversal separates the tense vowels from the vocalic optimum.

While reducing the time, the checked consonants increase their energy and thus attenuate the consonantal optimum. If a language possesses the two oppositions, checked/unchecked and tense/lax, then the optimal consonant, lax and unchecked, is opposed by two phonemes, the one checked (glottalized), the other tense. A double attenuation of the consonantal optimum may be further presented by the rare combination of two distinctive features, tense and checked within one and the same phoneme, such as the Avar /K'/.

Thus, all the inherent distinctive features actually rest upon two axes. On the one hand, the oppositions bearing upon the sonority axis display various fissions and attenuations of the primary contrast between optimal consonant and optimal vowel, and thus give rise to more minute and specific distinctions. On the other hand, those oppositions that involve the tonality axis, perpendicular to the sonority axis, emerge originally as the counterpart and corollary of the contrast, "optimal vowel *vs.* optimal consonant" and, subsequently, as the corollary of the opposition, "optimal, compact vowel *vs.* attenuated, diffuse vowel" or "optimal, diffuse consonant *vs.* attenuated, compact consonant".

4.2 *The dichotomous scale.* In their recent, quite autonomous development, phonemic analysis and the mathematical theory of communication arrived at fundamentally similar and mutually complementary conclusions, making possible a most productive cooperation on both sides.[31] Any spoken message presents the

[31] For procedures of the communication theory utilizable in phonemic analysis, see especially C. E. Shannon and W. Weaver, *The mathematical theory of communication* (Urbana, 1949); C. E. Shannon, 'The redundancy of English,' *Cybernetics*, Transactions of the Seventh Conference (New York, 1951); D. M. Mackay, 'In search of basic symbols,' *Cybernetics*, Transactions of the

listener with two complementary alignments of information: on the one hand, the chain of phonemes yields sequentially encoded information, on the other hand, every phoneme is composed of several distinctive features. The totality of these features is the minimum number of binary selections necessary for the specification of the phoneme. In reducing the phonemic information contained in the sequence to the smallest number of alternatives, we find the most economical and consequently the optimal solution: the minimum number of the simplest operations that would suffice to encode and decode the whole message. When analyzing a given language into its ultimate constituents, we seek the smallest set of distinctive oppositions which allow the identification of each phoneme in the messages framed in this language. This task requires an isolation of distinctive features from concurrent or adjoining redundant features.

If in a language, one and the same phoneme is implemented as a palatal stop before /i/, as a post-alveolar affricate before /e/ and as a velar stop in all other positions, the invariant must be determined as a compact (forward-flanged) consonant, distinct from the diffuse (backward-flanged) consonants /p/ and /t/ of the same language. While in such a case the redundant features are conditioned by the diverse distinctive features of the following phoneme, a striking example of redundant features linked to concurrent distinctive features may be found in the French consonantal pattern. Here, the compactness of the consonant is implemented by a velar articulation when lumped with plosiveness in /k/ and /g/, by a palatal articulation when lumped with nasality in /ɲ/, and by a post-alveolar articulation when lumped with constrictiveness in /ʃ/ and /ʒ/.

Such a delimitation of distinctive and redundant features not only permits an identification of all the phonemes involved but is

Eighth Conference (New York, 1952); D. Gabor, 'Lectures on communication theory,' M.I.T., Research Laboratory of Electronics, *Report*, No. 238 (1953); E. C. Cherry, *Human communication* (to be published by Wiley and Sons, together with The Technology Press). Cf. I. Pollack, 'Assimilation of sequentially encoded information,' *American Journal of Psychology*, LXVI (1953).

the unique solution, since any different analysis of these five
phonemes deviates from the optimal solution. All fifteen French
consonant phonemes in the proposed test require only five binary
decisions: nasal/oral, and if oral then continuant/discontinuous,
and tense/lax; compact/diffuse, and if diffuse then grave/acute.
Each French consonant contains from two (compact nasal) to five
distinctive features.

If one deemed the point of articulation distinctive, and the
difference between constrictive and stop redundant, then the six
French voiceless consonants – velar /k/, post-alveolar /ʃ/, alveolar
/s/, dental /t/, labiodental /f/ and bilabial /p/[32] – would require,
for their identification, fifteen distinctions instead of three,
according to the elementary mathematical formula cited by
Twaddell (1935): "If x is the maximum number of significant
phonological differentiations within a given articulatory range in
a language, then $2x = n (n - 1)$, where n is the maximum number
of phonemes in that range." Some of the minute differences in the
point of articulation have, moreover, the disadvantage of being
acoustically hardly recognizable by themselves. Finally, such
distinctions as /s/ *vs.* /f/ and /t/ *vs.* /p/ present an identical differential criterion, namely the opposition of an acute and grave consonant due to the same difference in the size and shape of the mouth
resonator. Also /k/ *vs.* /t/ and /ʃ/ *vs.* /s/ display (acoustically as
well as genetically) one and the same opposition, due to a parallel
relation of the front and back resonators, so that the operation
with the two pairs as if they were distinguished by two separate
features introduces superfluous redundancies.

The reduction of language into distinctive features must be
consistent. If, for instance, the Czech /l/, which can occur in
identical positions with each of the 32 other phonemes of the
language, is declared "an unanalyzable distinctive unit", its
distinction from the other 32 phonemes would require 32 unanalyzable relations, whereas the dissolution of the /l/ bundle into its
three features – vocalic, consonantal and continuous – reduces

---

[32]   See L. E. Armstrong, *The phonetics of French* (London, 1932).

its relation to all other phonemes of the pattern to three binary selections.

The maximum elimination of redundancies and the minimum amount of distinctive alternatives is a principle that permits an affirmative answer to the focal problem raised by Chao in 1934 on whether the task of breaking down a given language into its ultimate components yields a unique solution.[33] Not less crucial is his more recent question (1954), whether the dichotomous scale is the pivotal principle which the analyzer can profitably impose upon the linguistic code or whether this scale is inherent in the structure of language.[34] There are several weighty arguments in favor of the latter solution.

First, a system of distinctive features based on a mutually implicating relation between the terms of each binary opposition is the optimal code and it is unwarranted to assume that the speech participants in their encoding and decoding operations use a more complicated and less economic set of differential criteria. Recent experiments have disclosed that multidimensional auditory displays are most easily learned and perceived when "binary-coded".[35]

Second, the phonemic code is acquired in the earliest years of childhood and, as psychology reveals, in a child's mind the pair is anterior to isolated objects.[36] The binary opposition is a child's first logical operation. Both opposites arise simultaneously and force the infant to choose one and to suppress the other of the two alternative terms.

Third, almost all of the distinctive features show an unquestion-

[33] Y. R. Chao, 'The non-uniqueness of phonemic solution of phonetic systems,' Academia Sinica, Institute of History and Philology, *Bulletin*, IV (Shanghai, 1934).
[34] Y. R. Chao, review of Jakobson, Fant, Halle, *Preliminaries* ..., in *Romance Philology*, VIII (1954).
[35] I. Pollack and L. Ficks, 'Information of elementary multi-dimensional auditory displays,' *Journal of the Acoustical Society of America*, XXVI (1954).
[36] See H. Wallon, *Les origines de la pensée chez l'enfant*, I (Paris, 1945). For the pivotal role of gradual binary fissions in child development, cf. T. Parsons and R. F. Bales, *Family, socialization and interaction process* (Glencoe, 1955).

ably dichotomous structure on their acoustical and, correspondingly, on their motor level. Among the inherent features, only the vocalic distinction compact/diffuse often presents a higher number of terms, mostly three. For instance, /æ/ is to /e/ as /e/ is to /i/: the geometric mean /e/ is non-compact in relation to /æ/ and non-diffuse in relation to /i/. Psychological experiments that obtained /e/ through the mixture of /æ/ and /i/ confirm the peculiar structure of this vocalic feature.[37] Parallel experiments in mixing vowels situated on the tonality axis showed that grave and acute vowels, when sounded simultaneously, are not perceived as a single vowel: /u/ and /i/ do not merge into /y/. The feature grave/acute is a patently binary opposition. Since the second formant in /y/ is higher than in /u/ and lower than in /i/ and since in cavity length /y/ occupies a middle position in relation to /u/ with its longest, and /i/ with its shortest resonator, attempts were made to get along with one dimension for all three vowels.[38] But the chief genetic distinction is cardinally different: the disparity in the size of the lip orifice is primarily responsible for the relation /y/ vs. /i/, and the disparity in the size and shape of the resonator itself for the relation /y/ vs. /u/. On the acoustical level, the distinction of grave from acute in vowels is manifested in a relative proximity of the first and second formants which has, as a consequence, a very striking weakening of the upper formants, whereas the distinction of flat from plain is mainly due to the lowering in the second formant.[39]

[37] See K. Huber, 'Die Vokalmischung und das Qualitätensystem der Vokale,' *Archiv für Psychologie*, XCI (1934).

[38] See, e.g., F. Delattre, 'The physiological interpretation of sound spectrograms,' *PMLA*, LXVI (1951).

[39] Cf. Jakobson, Fant, Halle, *Preliminaries* ..., p. 48; H. K. Dunn, 'The calculation of vowel resonances, and an electrical vocal tract,' *Journal of the Acoustical Society of America*, XXII (1950), p. 650; K. N. Stevens and A. S. House, 'Development of a quantitative description of vowel articulation,' *ibidem*, XXVII (1955); detailed data are presented by Fant and Halle in the first volume of the series *The Structure of Contemporary Standard Russian* (to be published by Mouton & Co., The Hague).

[40] See especially L. Barczinski and E. Thienhaus, 'Klangspektren und Lautstärke deutscher Sprachlaute,' *Archives néerlandaises de phonétique expérimentale*, XI (1935).

Similarly, the effort to project the vocalic oppositions tense/lax and compact/diffuse upon one and the same line is hampered by the salient difference between their physical essence,[40] by the dissimilar parts they play in linguistic structure and by the considerable disadvantages which their unidimensional treatment imposes upon the analysis.

Finally, the application of the dichotomous scale makes the stratified structure of the phonemic patterns, their governing laws of implication, and the conclusive typology of languages so transparent that the inherence of this scale in the linguistic system is quite manifest.

4.3 *The spatio-temporal pattern of phonemic operations.* If there is a difference between the linguistic patterns of two speech communities, interlocution between members of the two communities demands an adjustment of the listener to the speaker and/or of the speaker to the listener. This adjustment may involve all aspects of language or only a few of them. Sometimes the phonemic code is the only one affected. Both on the listener's and on the speaker's side there are different degrees of this adjustment process, neatly called code switching by the communication engineers. The receiver in trying to understand the sender, and/or the sender in trying to make himself understood, concentrate their attention on the common core of their codes. A higher degree of adjustment is represented in the effort to overcome the phonemic differences by switching rules, heightening the intelligibility of the message for its addressee. Having found these clues, the interlocutor may try to use them not only as a listener, but also more actively, in adapting his own utterances to the pattern of his addressee.

The phonemic adjustment may cover the whole lexical stock or the imitation of the neighbor's phonemic code may be confined to a certain set of words directly borrowed from the neighbor or at least particularly stamped by his use of them. Whatever the adjustments are, they help the speaker to increase the radius of communication, and if often practiced, they are likely to enter into his everyday language. Under favorable circumstances they may subsequently infiltrate into the general use of the speech community, either as a particular speech fashion or as a new pattern fully substituted for the former norm. Interdialectal communication and its influence on intradialectal communication must be analyzed from a linguistic and, particularly, from a phonemic point of view.[41]

The problem of bridging space stops neither at the borders of distant and highly differentiated dialects, nor at the boundaries of related or even unrelated languages. Mediators, more or less bilingual, adapt themselves to the foreign phonemic code. Their prestige grows with the widening radius of their audience and may further a diffusion of their innovations among their monolingual tribesmen.

Not only the interdialectal, but also the interlingual adjustment may affect the phonemic code without limitation to borrowed words or even without any lexical borrowing. In all parts of the world, linguists have been surprised, as Sapir confesses, to observe "the remarkable fact that distinctive phonetic features tend to be distributed over wide areas regardless of the vocabularies and structures of the languages involved."[42] This far-reaching phenomenon still awaits systematic mapping and study in connection with the equally urgent inquiry into the typology of phonemic patterns.

The other possibility of phonemic adjustments to a different dialect or foreign language is a partial or total preservation of its phonemic structure in borrowed words. As noted repeatedly in phonemic literature, and closely examined by Fries and Pike, "the speech of monolingual natives of some languages is comprised of more than one phonemic system."[43] Such a coexistence of two systems within one language is due either to a phonemic difference between the original vocabulary and unassimilated loanwords, or

---

[41] See 'Results of the Conference of Anthropologists and Linguists,' *Indiana University Publications in Anthropology and Linguistics*, VIII (1953), pp. 16 f., 36ff.

[42] S. Sapir, 'Language,' *Selected Writings* (Berkeley and Los Angeles, 1949), p. 25.

[43] C. C. Fries and K. L. Pike, 'Coexistent phonemic systems,' *Language*, XXV (1949).

to the use of two patterns, one native and the other imitative, as different styles of speech. Thus phenomena of space, namely interdialectal or interlingual isoglosses, especially isophones, may be projected into the framework of a single dialect, individual or social.

The same statement, *mutatis mutandis*, may be made about the time factor in language, particularly in the phonemic field. Any sound change in progress is a synchronic fact. Both the start and the finish of a change coexist for a certain length of time. If the change differentiates the younger generation from the older, there is always some intercourse between the two generations, and the receiver belonging to one is accustomed to recode messages from a sender of the other. Furthermore, the initial and the final stage may co-occur in the use of one and the same generation as two stylistic levels: on the one hand, a more conservative and solemn, on the other, a more fashionable way of talking. Thus synchronic analysis must encompass linguistic changes and, *vice versa*, linguistic changes may be comprehended only in the light of synchronic analysis.

The decisive factor in phonemic changes and in the diffusion of phonemic phenomena is the shift in the code. The interpretation of events in time and space is primarily concerned with the question in what respect the structure of the code is affected by such shifts. The motor and physical aspects of these innovations cannot be treated as self-sufficient agents, but must be subordinated to the strictly linguistic analysis of their role in the coding system.

TWO ASPECTS OF LANGUAGE AND TWO TYPES OF APHASIC DISTURBANCES

BY

ROMAN JAKOBSON

APHASIA AS A LINGUISTIC PROBLEM

If aphasia is a language disturbance, as the term itself suggests then any description and classification of aphasic syndromes must begin with the question of what aspects of language are impaired in the various species of such a disorder. This problem, which was approached long ago by Hughlings Jackson,[1] cannot be solved without the participation of professional linguists familiar with the patterning and functioning of language. To study adequately any breakdown in communications we must first understand the nature and structure of the particular mode of communication that has ceased to function. Linguistics is concerned with language in all its aspects – language in operation, language in drift,[2] language in the nascent state, and language in dissolution.

At present there are psychopathologists who assign a high importance to the linguistic problems involved in the study of language disturbances;[3] some of these questions have been touched upon in the best recent treatises on aphasia.[4] And yet, in most cases, this valid insistence on the linguists' contribution to the investigation of aphasia is still ignored. For instance, a new book dealing to a

[1] Hughlings Jackson, Papers on affections of speech (reprinted and commented by H. Head), *Brain*, XXXVIII (1915).

[2] E. Sapir, *Language* (New York, 1921), Chapter VII: 'Language as a historical product; drift.'

[3] See, for instance, the discussion on aphasia in the Nederlandsche Vereeniging voor Phonetische Wetenschappen with papers by the linguist J. van Ginneken and by two psychiatrists, F. Grewel and V. W. D. Schenk, *Psychiatrische en Neurologische Bladen*, XLV (1941), p. 1035ff.; cf. furthermore, F. Grewel, 'Aphasie en linguistiek,' *Nederlandsch Tijdschrift voor Geneeskunde*, XCIII (1949), p. 726ff.

[4] A. R. Luria, *Travmatičeskaja afazija* (Moscow, 1947); Kurt Goldstein, *Language and language disturbances* (New York, 1948); André Ombredane, *L'aphasie et l'élaboration de la pensée explicite* (Paris, 1951).

great extent with the complex and intricate problems of infantile aphasia, calls for a coordination of various disciplines and appeals for cooperation to otolaryngologists, pediatricians, audiologists, psychiatrists, and educators; but the science of language is passed over in silence, as if disorders in speech perception had nothing whatever to do with language.[5] This omission is the more deplorable since the author is Director of the Child Hearing and Aphasia Clinics at Northwestern University, which counts among its linguists Werner F. Leopold, by far the best American expert in child language.

The linguists are also responsible for the delay in undertaking a joint inquiry into aphasia. Nothing comparable to the minute linguistic observations of infants of various countries has been performed with respect to aphasics. Nor has there been any attempt to re-interpret and systematize from the point of view of linguistics the multifarious clinical data on diverse types of aphasia. That this should be true is all the more surprising in view of the fact that, on the one hand, the amazing progress of structural linguistics has endowed the investigator with efficient tools and methods for the study of verbal regression and, on the other, the aphasic disintegration of the verbal pattern may provide the linguist with new insights into the general laws of language.

The application of purely linguistic criteria to the interpretation and classification of aphasic facts may substantially contribute to the science of language and language disturbances, provided that linguists remain as careful and cautious when dealing with psychological and neurological data as they have been in their traditional field. First of all, they should be familiar with the technical terms and devices of the medical disciplines dealing with aphasia, then they must submit the clinical case reports to thorough linguistic analysis, and, further, they should themselves work with aphasic patients in order to approach the cases directly and not only through a re-interpretation of prepared records which have been quite differently conceived and elaborated.

---

[5] H. Myklebust, *Auditory disorders in children* (New York, 1954).

There is one level of aphasic phenomena where amazing agreement has been achieved during the last twenty years between those psychiatrists and linguists who have tackled these problems, namely the disintegration of the sound pattern.[6] This dissolution exhibits a time order of great regularity. Aphasie regression has proved to be a mirror of the child's acquisition of speech sounds, it shows the child's development in reverse. Furthermore, comparison of child language and aphasia enables us to establish several laws of implication. This search for the order of acquisitions and losses and for the general laws of implication cannot be confined to the phonemic pattern but must be extended also to the grammatical system. Only a few tentative trials have been made in this direction, and these efforts deserve to be continued.[7]

[6] The aphasic impoverishment of the sound pattern was observed and discussed by the linguist Marguerite Durand together with the psychopathologists Th. Alajouanine and A. Ombredane (in their common work *Le syndrome de désintégration phonétique dans l'aphasie*, Paris, 1939) and by R. Jakobson (the first draft presented to the International Congress of Linguists at Brussels in 1939 – see N. Trubetzkoy, *Principes de phonologie*, Paris, 1949, pp. 367-79 – was later developed into an outline, 'Kindersprache, Aphasie und allgemeine Lautgesetze,' *Uppsala Universitets Årsskrift*, 1942 : 9) and has been further studied in his *Sound and Meaning* (to be published by Wiley and Sons, together with The Technology Press). Cf. K. Goldstein, p. 32ff.

[7] A joint inquiry into certain grammatical disturbances was undertaken at the Bonn University Clinic by a linguist, G. Kandler, and two physicians, F. Panse and A. Leischner: see their report, *Klinische und sprachwissenschaftliche Untersuchungen zum Agrammatismus* (Stuttgart, 1952).

THE TWOFOLD CHARACTER OF LANGUAGE

Speech implies a selection of certain linguistic entities and their combination into linguistic units of a higher degree of complexity. At the lexical level this is readily apparent: the speaker selects words and combines them into sentences according to the syntactic system of the language he is using; sentences are in their turn combined into utterances. But the speaker is by no means a completely free agent in his choice of words: his selection (except for the rare case of actual neology) must be made from the lexical storehouse which he and his addressee possess in common. The communication engineer most properly approaches the essence of the speech event when he assumes that in the optimal exchange of information the speaker and the listener have at their disposal more or less the same "filing cabinet of *prefabricated* representations": the addresser of a verbal message selects one of these "preconceived possibilities" and the addressee is supposed to make an identical choice from the same assembly of "possibilities already foreseen and provided for".[8] Thus the efficiency of a speech event demands the use of a common code by its participants.

"'Did you say *pig* or *fig*?' said the Cat. 'I said *pig*,' replied Alice."[9] In this peculiar utterance the feline addressee attempts to recapture a linguistic choice made by the addresser. In the common code of the Cat and Alice, i.e. in spoken English, the difference between a stop and a continuant, other things being equal, may change the meaning of the message. Alice had used the distinctive feature "stop *vs.* continuant", rejecting the latter and choosing the former of the two opposites; and in the same act

[8] D. M. MacKay, 'In search of basic symbols,' *Cybernetics*, Transactions of the Eighth Conference (New York, 1952), p. 183.
[9] Lewis Carroll, *Alice's adventures in Wonderland*, Chapter VI.

of speech she combined this solution with certain other simultaneous features, using the gravity and the tenseness of /p/ in contradistinction to the acuteness of /t/ and to the laxness of /b/. Thus all these attributes have been combined into a bundle of distinctive features, the so-called p h o n e m e. The phoneme /p/ was then f o l l o w e d by the phonemes /i/ and /g/, themselves bundles of simultaneously produced distinctive features. Hence the c o n-c u r r e n c e of simultaneous entities and the c o n c a t e n a t i o n of successive entities are the two ways in which we speakers combine linguistic constituents.

Neither such bundles as /p/ or /f/ nor such sequences of bundles as /pig/ or /fig/ are invented by the speaker who uses them. Neither can the distinctive feature "stop *versus* continuant" nor the phoneme /p/ occur out of a context. The stop feature appears in combination with certain other concurrent features, and the repertory of combinations of these features into phonemes such as /p/, /b/, /t/, /d/, /k/, /g/, etc. is limited by the code of the given language. The code sets limitations on the possible combinations of the phoneme /p/ with other following and/or preceding phonemes; and only a part of the permissible phoneme-sequences are actually utilized in the lexical stock of a given language. Even when other combinations of phonemes are theoretically possible, the speaker, as a rule, is only a word-user, not a word-coiner. When facing with individual words, we expect them to be coded units. In order to grasp the word *nylon* one must know the meaning assigned to this vocable in the lexical code of modern English.

In any language, there exist also coded word-groups called p h r a s e - w o r d s. The meaning of the idiom *how do you do* cannot be derived by adding together the meanings of its lexical constituents; the whole is not equal to the sum of its parts. Those word-groups which in this respect behave like single words are a common but nonetheless only marginal case. In order to comprehend the overwhelming majority of word-groups, we must be familiar only with the constituent words and with the syntactical rules of their combination. Within these limitations we are free to set words in new contexts. Of course, this freedom is relative, and the pressure of current clichés upon our choice of combinations is considerable. But the freedom to compose quite new contexts is undeniable, despite the relatively low statistical probability of their occurrence.

Thus in the combination of linguistic units there is an ascending scale of freedom. In the combination of distinctive features into phonemes, the freedom of the individual speaker is zero; the code has already established all the possibilities which may be utilized in the given language. Freedom to combine phonemes into words is circumscribed, it is limited to the marginal situation of word-coinage. In the forming of sentences out of words the speaker is less constrained. And finally, in the combination of sentences into utterances, the action of compulsory syntactical rules ceases and the freedom of any individual speaker to create novel contexts increases substantially, although again the numerous stereotyped utterances are not to be overlooked.

Any linguistic sign involves two modes of arrangement.

1) Combination. Any sign is made up of constituent signs and/or occurs only in combination with other signs. This means that any linguistic unit at one and the same time serves as a context for simpler units and/or finds its own context in a more complex linguistic unit. Hence any actual grouping of linguistic units binds them into a superior unit: combination and contexture are two faces of the same operation.

2) Selection. A selection between alternatives implies the possibility of substituting one for the other, equivalent to the former in one respect and different from it in another. Actually, selection and substitution are two faces of the same operation.

The fundamental role which these two operations play in language was clearly realized by Ferdinand de Saussure. Yet from the two varieties of combination – concurrence and concatenation – it was only the latter, the temporal sequence, which was recognized by the Geneva linguist. Despite his own insight into the phoneme as a set of concurrent distinctive features (*éléments différentiels des phonèmes*), the scholar succumbed to the traditional belief in the linear character of language *"qui exclut la possibilité de prononcer deux éléments à la fois".*[10]

In order to delimit the two modes of arrangement which we have described as combination and selection, F. de Saussure states that the former "is *in presentia:* it is based on two or several terms jointly present in an actual series," whereas the latter "connects terms *in absentia* as members of a virtual mnemonic series". That is to say, selection (and, correspondingly, substitution) deals with entities conjoined in the code but not in the given message, whereas, in the case of combination, the entities are conjoined in both or only in the actual message. The addressee perceives that the given utterance (message) is a combination of constituent parts (sentences, words, phonemes, etc.) selected from the repository of all possible constituent parts (code). The constituents of a context are in a status of contiguity, while in a substitution set signs are linked by various degrees of similarity which fluctuate between the equivalence of synonyms and the common core of antonyms.

These two operations provide each linguistic sign with two sets of interpretants, to utilize the effective concept introduced by Charles Sanders Peirce:[11] there are two references which serve to interpret the sign – one to the code, and the other to the context, whether coded or free; and in each of these ways the sign is related to another set of linguistic signs, through an alternation in the former case and through an alignment in the latter. A given significative unit may be replaced by other, more explicit signs of the same code, whereby its general meaning is revealed, while its contextual meaning is determined by its connection with other signs within the same sequence.

The constituents of any message are necessarily linked with the code by an internal relation and with the message by an external relation. Language in its various aspects deals with both modes of

[10] F. de Saussure, *Cours de linguistique générale*, 2nd ed. (Paris, 1922), pp. 68f. and 170f.

[11] C. S. Peirce, *Collected Papers*, II and IV (Cambridge, Mass., 1932, 1934) – see Index of subjects.

relation. Whether messages are exchanged or communication proceeds unilaterally from the addresser to the addressee, there must be some kind of contiguity between the participants of any speech event to assure the transmission of the message. The separation in space, and often in time, between two individuals, the addresser and the addressee, is bridged by an internal relation: there must be a certain equivalence between the symbols used by the addresser and those known and interpreted by the addressee. Without such an equivalence the message is fruitless – even when it reaches the receiver it does not affect him.

SIMILARITY DISORDER

It is clear that speech disturbances may affect in varying degrees the individual's capacity for combination and selection of linguistic units, and indeed the question of which of these two operations is chiefly impaired proves to be of far-reaching significance in describing, analyzing and classifying the diverse forms of aphasia. This dichotomy is perhaps even more suggestive than the classical distinction (not discussed in this paper) between emissive and receptive aphasia, indicating which of the two functions in speech exchange, the encoding or the decoding of verbal messages, is particularly affected.

Head attempted to classify cases of aphasia into definite groups,[12] and to each of these varieties he assigned "a name chosen to signify the most salient defect in the management and comprehension of words and phrases" (p. 412). Following this device, we distinguish two basic types of aphasia – depending on whether the major deficiency lies in selection and substitution, with relative stability of combination and contexture; or conversely, in combination and contexture, with relative retention of normal selection and substitution. In outlining these two opposite patterns of aphasia, I shall utilize mainly Goldstein's data.

For aphasics of the first type (selection deficiency), the context is the indispensable and decisive factor. When presented with scraps of words or sentences, such a patient readily completes them. His speech is merely reactive: he easily carries on conversation, but has difficulties in starting a dialogue; he is able to reply to a real or imaginary addresser when he is, or imagines himself to be the addressee of the message. It is particularly hard for him to

[12]   H. Head, *Aphasia and kindred disorders of speech,* I (New York, 1926).

perform, or even to understand, such a closed discourse as the monologue. The more his utterances are dependent on the context, the better he copes with his verbal task. He feels unable to utter a sentence which responds neither to the cue of his interlocutor nor to the actual situation. The sentence "it rains" cannot be produced unless the utterer sees that it is actually raining. The deeper the utterance is embedded in the verbal or non-verbalized context, the higher are the chances of its successful performance by this class of patients.

Likewise, the more a word is dependent on the other words of the same sentence and the more it refers to the syntactical context, the less it is affected by the speech disturbance. Therefore words syntactically subordinated by grammatical agreement or government are more tenacious, whereas the main subordinating agent of the sentence, namely the subject, tends to be omitted. As long as any start is the main obstacle for the patient, it is obvious that he will fail precisely at the starting point, the cornerstone of the sentence-pattern. In this type of language disturbance, sentences are conceived as elliptical sequels to be supplied from antecedent sentences uttered, if not imagined, by the aphasic himself, or received by him from the other partner of the colloquy, actual if not imaginary. Key words may be dropped or superseded by abstract anaphoric substitutes.[13] A specific noun, as Freud noticed, is replaced by a very general one, for instance *machin, chose* in the speech of French aphasics.[14] In a dialectal German sample of "amnesic aphasia" observed by Goldstein (p. 246ff.), *Ding* 'thing' or *Stückle* 'piece' were substituted for all inanimate nouns, and *überfahren* 'perform' for verbs which were identifiable from the context or situation and therefore appeared superfluous to the patient.

Words with an inherent reference to the context, like pronouns and pronominal adverbs, and words serving merely to construct the context, such as connectives and auxiliaries, are particularly

---

[13]   Cf. L. Bloomfield, *Language* (New York, 1933), Chapter XV: Substitution.

[14]   S. Freud, *On aphasia* (London, 1953), p. 22.

prone to survive. A typical utterance of a German patient, recorded by Quensel and quoted by Goldstein (p. 302) will serve as illustration:

„Ich bin doch hier unten, na wenn ich gewesen bin ich wees nicht, we das, nu wenn ich, ob das nun doch, noch, ja. Was Sie her, wenn ich, och ich weess nicht, we das hier war ja..."

Thus only the framework, the connecting links of communication, is spared by this type of aphasia at its critical stage.

In the theory of language since the early Middle Ages, it has repeatedly been asserted that the word out of context has no meaning. The validity of this statement is, however, confined to aphasia, or more exactly to one type of aphasia. In the pathological cases under discussion an isolated word means actually nothing but "blab". As numerous tests have disclosed, for such patients two occurrences of the same word in two different contexts are mere homonyms. Since distinctive vocables carry a higher amount of information than homonyms, some aphasics of this type tend to supplant the contextual variants of one word by different terms, each of them specific for the given environment. Thus Goldstein's patient never uttered the word *knife* alone, but according to its use and surroundings, alternately called the knife *pencil-sharpener*, *apple-parer*, *bread-knife*, *knife-and-fork* (p. 62); so that the word *knife* was changed from a free form, capable of occurring alone, into a bound form.

"I have a good apartment, entrance hall, bedroom, kitchen," Goldstein's patient says. "There are also big apartments, only in the rear live bachelors." A more explicit form, the word-group *unmarried people*, could have been substituted for *bachelors*, but this univerbal term was selected by the speaker. When repeatedly asked what a bachelor was, the patient did not answer and was "apparently in distress" (p. 270). A reply like "a bachelor is an unmarried man" or "an unmarried man is a bachelor" would present an equational predication and thus a projection of a substitution set from the lexical code of the English language into the context of the given message. The equivalent terms become two

correlated parts of the sentence and consequently are tied by
contiguity. The patient was able to select the appropriate term
bachelor when it was supported by the context of a customary
conversation about "bachelor apartments", but was incapable of
utilizing the substitution set *bachelor = unmarried man* as the topic
of a sentence, because the ability for autonomous selection and
substitution had been affected. The equational sentence vainly
demanded from the patient carries as its sole information:
"«bachelor» means an unmarried man" or "an unmarried man is
called «bachelor»".

The same difficulty arises when the patient is asked to name an
object pointed to or handled by the examiner. The aphasic with a
defect in substitution will not supplement the pointing or handling
gesture of the examiner with the name of the object pointed to.
Instead of saying "this is [called] a pencil," he will merely add an
elliptical note about its use: "To write." If one of the synonymic
signs is present (as for instance the word *bachelor* or the pointing
to the pencil) then the other sign (such as the phrase *unmarried
man* or the word *pencil*) becomes redundant and consequently
superfluous. For the aphasic, both signs are in complementary
distribution: if one is performed by the examiner, the patient will
avoid its synonym: "I understand everything" or "Ich weiss es
schon" will be his typical reaction. Likewise, the picture of an object
will cause suppression of its name: a verbal sign is supplanted by a
pictorial sign. When the picture of a compass was presented to a
patient of Lotmar's, he responded: "Yes, it's a ... I know what
it belongs to, but I cannot recall the technical expression ... Yes ...
direction ... to show direction ... a magnet points to the north."[15]
Such patients fail to shift, as Peirce would say, from an index or
icon to a corresponding verbal symbol.[16]

Even simple repetition of a word uttered by the examiner seems

---

[15] F. Lotmar, 'Zur Pathophysiologie der erschwerten Wortfindung bei
Aphasischen,' *Schweiz. Archiv für Neurologie und Psychiatrie*, XXXV (1933),
p. 104.

[16] C. S. Peirce, 'The icon, index and symbol,' *Collected papers*, II (Cambridge, Mass., 1932).

to the patient unnecessarily redundant, and despite instructions received he is unable to repeat it. Told to repeat the word "no," Head's patient replied "No, I don't know how to do it." While spontaneously using the word in the context of his answer ("No, I don't ..."), he could not produce the purest form of equational predication, the tautology a = a: «no» is «no».

One of the important contributions of symbolic logic to the science of language is its emphasis on the distinction between object language and metalanguage. As Carnap states, "in order to speak *about* any *object language*, we need a *metalanguage*."[17] On these two different levels of language the same linguistic stock may be used; thus we may speak in English (as metalanguage) about English (as object language) and interpret English words and sentences by means of English synonyms, circumlocutions and paraphrases. Obviously such operations, labeled metalinguistic by the logicians, are not their invention: far from being confined to the sphere of science, they prove to be an integral part of our customary linguistic activities. The participants in a dialogue often check whether both of them are using the same code. "Do you follow? Do you see what I mean?", the speaker asks, or the listener himself breaks in with "What do you mean?" Then, by replacing the questionable sign with another sign from the same linguistic code, or with a whole group of code signs, the sender of the message seeks to make it more accessible to the decoder.

The interpretation of one linguistic sign through other, in some respect homogeneous signs of the same language, is a metalinguistic operation which also plays an essential role in child language learning. Recent observations have disclosed what a considerable place talk about language occupies in the verbal behavior of preschool children. Recourse to metalanguage is necessary both for the acquisition of language and for its normal functioning. The aphasic defect in the "capacity of naming" is properly a loss of metalanguage. As a matter of fact, the examples of equational predication sought in vain from the patients cited above, are meta-

---

[17] R. Carnap, *Meaning and necessity* (Chicago, 1947), p. 4.

linguistic propositions referring to the English language. Their explicit wording would be: "In the code that we use, the name of the indicated object is «pencil»"; or "In the code we use, the word «bachelor» and the circumlocution «unmarried man» are equivalent."

Such an aphasic can neither switch from a word to its synonyms and circumlocutions, nor to its heteronyms, i.e. equivalent expressions in other languages. Loss of a polyglot ability and confinement to a single dialectal variety of a single language is a symptomatic manifestation of this disorder.

According to an old but recurrent bias, a single individual's way of speaking at a given time, labeled idiolect, has been viewed as the only concrete linguistic reality. In the discussion of this concept the following objections were raised:

Everyone, when speaking to a new person, tries, deliberately or involuntarily, to hit upon a common vocabulary: either to please or simply to be understood or, finally, to bring him out, he uses the terms of his addressee. There is no such thing as private property in language: everything is socialized. Verbal exchange, like any form of intercourse, requires at least two communicators, and idiolect proves to be a somewhat perverse fiction.[18]

This statement needs, however, one reservation: for an aphasic who has lost the capacity of code switching, his "idiolect" indeed becomes the sole linguistic reality. As long as he does not regard another's speech as a message addressed to him in his own verbal pattern, he feels, as a patient of Hemphil and Stengel expressed it: "I can hear you dead plain but I cannot get what you say ... I hear your voice but not the words ... It does not pronounce itself."[19] He considers the other's utterance to be either gibberish or at least in an unknown language.

As noted above, it is the external relation of contiguity which unites the constituents of a context, and the internal relation of

[18] 'Results of the Conference of Anthropologists and Linguists,' *Indiana University Publications in Anthropology and Linguistics*, VIII (1953), p. 15.

[19] R. E. Hemphil and E. Stengel, 'Pure word deafness,' *Journal of Neurology and Psychiatry*, III (1940), pp. 251-62.

similarity which underlies the substitution set. Hence for an aphasic with impaired substitution and intact contexture, operations involving similarity yield to those based on contiguity. It could be predicted that under these conditions any semantic grouping would be guided by spatial or temporal contiguity rather than by similarity. Actually Goldstein's tests justify such an expectation: a female patient of this type, when asked to list a few names of animals, disposed them in the same sequence in which she had seen them in the zoo; similarly, despite instructions to arrange certain objects according to color, size and shape, she classified them on the basis of their spatial contiguity as home things, office materials, etc. and justified this grouping by a reference to a show window where "it does not matter what the things are," i.e. they do not have to be similar (pp. 61f., 263ff.). The same patient was willing to name the primary hues – red, blue, green and yellow – but declined to extend these names to the transitional varieties (p. 268f.), since, for her, words had no capacity to assume additional, shifted meanings associated by similarity with their primary meaning.

One must agree with Goldstein's observation that patients of this type "grasped the words in their literal meaning but could not be brought to understand the metaphoric character of the same words" (p. 270). It would, however, be an unwarranted generalization to assume that figurative speech is altogether incomprehensible to them. From the two polar figures of speech, metaphor and metonymy, the latter, based on contiguity, is widely employed by aphasics whose selective capacities have been affected. *Fork* is substituted for *knife*, *table* for *lamp*, *smoke* for *pipe*, *eat* for *toaster*. A typical case is reported by Head:

When he failed to recall the name for "black", he described it as "What you do for the dead"; this he shortened to "dead" (I, p. 198).

Such metonymies may be characterized as projections from the line of a habitual context into the line of substitution and selection: a sign (e.g. *fork*) which usually occurs together with another sign (e.g. *knife*) may be used instead of this sign. Phrases like "knife and fork", "table lamp", "to smoke a pipe", induced the metonymies *fork, table, smoke;* the relation between the use of an object (toast) and the means of its production underlies the metonymy *eat* for *toaster.* "When does one wear black?" – "When mourning for the dead": in place of naming the color, the cause of its traditional use is designated. The escape from sameness to contiguity is particularly striking in such cases as Goldstein's patient who would answer with a metonymy when asked to repeat a given word and, for instance, would say *glass* for *window* and *heaven* for *God* (p. 280).

When the selective capacity is strongly impaired and the gift for combination at least partly preserved, then contiguity determines the patients' whole verbal behavior, and we may designate this type of aphasia similarity disorder.

CONTIGUITY DISORDER

From 1864 on it was repeatedly pointed out in Hughlings Jackson's pioneer contributions to the modern study of language and language disturbances:

It is not enough to say that speech consists of words. It consists of words referring to one another in a particular manner; and, without a proper interrelation of its parts, a verbal utterance would be a mere succession of names embodying no proposition (p. 66).[20]

Loss of speech is the loss of power to propositionize... Speechlessness does not mean entire wordlessness (p. 114).[21]

The impairment of the ability to propositionize, or generally speaking, to combine simpler linguistic entities into more complex units, is actually confined to one type of aphasia, the opposite of the type discussed in the preceding chapter. There is no word-lessness, since the entity preserved in most of such cases is the word, which can be defined as the highest among the linguistic units compulsorily coded, i.e., we compose our own sentences and utterances out of the word stock supplied by the code.

This contexture-deficient aphasia, which could be termed contiguity disorder, diminishes the extent and variety of sentences. The syntactical rules organizing words into a higher unit are lost; this loss, called agrammatism, causes the degeneration of the sentence into a mere "word heap", to use Jackson's image.[22] Word order becomes chaotic; the ties of grammatical

[20] H. Jackson, 'Notes on the physiology and pathology of the nervous system' (1868), *Brain*, XXXVIII (1915), pp. 65-71.

[21] H. Jackson, 'On affections of speech from disease of the brain' (1879), *Brain*, XXXVIII (1915), pp. 107-29.

[22] H. Jackson, 'Notes on the physiology and pathology of language' (1866), *Brain*, XXXVIII (1915), pp. 48-58.

coordination and subordination, whether concord or government, are dissolved. As might be expected, words endowed with purely grammatical functions, like conjunctions, prepositions, pronouns, and articles, disappear first, giving rise to the so-called "telegraphic style", whereas in the case of similarity disorder they are the most resistant. The less a word depends grammatically on the context, the stronger is its tenacity in the speech of aphasics with a contiguity disorder and the sooner is it dropped by patients with a similarity disorder. Thus the "kernel subject word" is the first to fall out of the sentence in cases of similarity disorder and, conversely, it is the least destructible in the opposite type of aphasia.

The aphasia affecting contexture tends to infantile one-sentence utterances and one-word sentences. Only a few longer, stereotyped, "ready made" sentences manage to survive. In advanced cases of this disease, each utterance is reduced to a single one-word sentence. While contexture disintegrates, the selective operation goes on. "To say what a thing is, is to say what it is like," Jackson notes (p. 125). The patient confined to the substitution set (once contexture is deficient) deals with similarities, and his approximate identifications are of a metaphoric nature, contrary to the metonymie ones familiar to the opposite type of aphasics. *Spyglass* for *microscope*, or *fire* for *gaslight* are typical examples of such quasi-metaphoric expressions, as Jackson christened them, since, in contradistinction to rhetoric or poetic metaphors, they present no deliberate transfer of meaning.

In a normal language pattern, the w o r d is at the same time both a constituent part of a superimposed context, the s e n t e n c e, and itself a context superimposed on ever smaller constituents, m o r p h e m e s (minimum units endowed with meaning) and p h o n e m e s. We have discussed the effect of contiguity disorder on the combination of words into higher units. The relationship between the word and its constituents reflects the same impairment, yet in a somewhat different way. A typical feature of agrammatism is the abolition of inflection: there appear such u n m a r k e d categories as the infinitive in place of diverse finite verbal forms, and in languages with declension, the nominative instead of all the oblique cases. These defects are due partly to the elimination of government and concord, partly to the loss of ability to dissolve words into stem and desinence. Finally, a paradigm (in particular a set of grammatical cases such as *he – his – him*, or of tenses such as *he votes – he voted*) presents the same semantic content from different viewpoints associated with each other by contiguity; so there is one more impetus for aphasics with a contiguity disorder to dismiss such sets.

Also, as a rule, words derived from the same root, such as *grant – grantor – grantee* are semantically related by contiguity. The patients under discussion are either inclined to drop the derivative words, or the combination of a root with a derivational suffix and even a compound of two words become irresolvable for them. Patients who understood and uttered such compounds as *Thanks-giving* or *Battersea*, but were unable to grasp or to say *thanks* and *giving* or *batter* and *sea*, have often been cited. As long as the sense of derivation is still alive, so that this process is still used for creating innovations in the code, there can be observed a tendency toward oversimplification and automatism: if the derivative word constitutes a semantic unit which cannot be entirely inferred from the meaning of its components, the Gestalt is misunderstood. Thus the Russian word *mokr-íca* signifies 'wood-louse', but a Russian aphasic interpreted it as 'something humid', especially 'humid weather', since the root *mokr-* means 'humid' and the suffix *-ica* designates a carrier of the given property, as in *nelépica* 'something absurd', *svetlíca* 'light room', *temnica* 'dungeon' (literally 'dark room').

When, before the Word War II, phonemics was the most controversial area in the science of language, doubts were expressed by some linguists as to whether phonemes really play an autonomous part in our verbal behavior. It was even suggested that the meaningful (significative) units of the linguistic code, such as morphemes or sooner words, are the minimal entities with which we actually deal in a speech event, whereas the merely distinctive units, such as phonemes, are an artificial construct to facilitate the scientific description and analysis of a language.

This view, which was stigmatized by Sapir as "the reverse of realistic",[23] remains, however, perfectly valid with respect to a certain pathological type: in one variety of aphasia which sometimes was labeled "atactic", the word is the sole linguistic unity preserved. The patient has only an integral, indissolvable image of any familiar word, and all other sound-sequences are either alien and inscrutable to him or he merges them into familiar words by disregarding their phonetic aberrations. One of Goldstein's patients "perceived some words, but . . . the vowels and consonants of which they consisted were not perceived" (p. 218). A French aphasic recognized, understood, repeated, and spontaneously produced the word *café* 'coffee' or *pavé* 'roadway', but was unable to grasp, discern, or repeat such nonsensical sequences as *féca*, *faké*, *kéfa*, *pafé*. None of these difficulties exists for a normal French-speaking listener as long as the sound-sequences and their components fit the French phonemic pattern. Such a listener may even apprehend these sequences as words unknown to him but plausibly belonging to the French vocabulary and presumably different in meaning, since they differ from each other either in the order of their phonemes or in the phonemes themselves.

If an aphasic becomes unable to resolve the word into its phonemic constituents, his control over its construction weakens, and perceptible damages in phonemes and their combinations easily follow. The gradual regression of the sound pattern in aphasics regularly reverses the order of children's phonemic acquisitions. This regression involves an inflation of homonyms and a decrease of vocabulary. If this twofold – phonemic and lexical – disablement progresses further, the last residues of speech are one-phoneme – one-word – one-sentence utterances: the patient relapses into the initial phases of infants' linguistic development or even to their pre-lingual stage: he faces *aphasia universalis*, the total loss of the power to use or apprehend speech.

The separateness of the two functions – one distinctive and the other significative – is a peculiar feature of language as compared

[23]   E. Sapir, 'The psychological reality of phonemes,' *Selected writings* (Berkeley and Los Angeles, 1949), p. 46ff.

to other semiotic systems. There arises a conflict between these two levels of language when the aphasic deficient in contexture exhibits a tendency to abolish the hierarchy of linguistic units and to reduce their scale to a single level. The last level to remain is either a class of significative values, the w o r d, as in the cases touched upon, or a class of distinctive values, the p h o n e m e. In the latter case the patient is still able to identify, distinguish and reproduce phonemes, but loses the capacity to do the same with words. In an intermediate case, words are identified, distinguished and reproduced; according to Goldstein's acute formulation, they "may be grasped as known but not understood" (p. 90). Here the word loses its normal significative function and assumes the purely distinctive function which normally pertains to the phoneme.

THE METAPHORIC AND METONYMIC POLES

The varieties of aphasia are numerous and diverse, but all of them oscillate between the two polar types just described. Every form of aphasic disturbance consists in some impairment, more or less severe, either of the faculty for selection and substitution or for combination and contexture. The former affliction involves a deterioration of metalinguistic operations, while the latter damages the capacity for maintaining the hierarchy of linguistic units. The relation of similarity is suppressed in the former, the relation of contiguity in the latter type of aphasia. Metaphor is alien to the similarity disorder, and metonymy to the contiguity disorder.

The development of a discourse may take place along two different semantic lines: one topic may lead to another either through their similarity or through their contiguity. The metaphoric way would be the most appropriate term for the first case and the metonymic way for the second, since they find their most condensed expression in metaphor and metonymy respectively. In aphasia one or the other of these two processes is restricted or totally blocked – an effect which makes the study of aphasia particularly illuminating for the linguist. In normal verbal behavior both processes are continually operative, but careful observation will reveal that under the influence of a cultural pattern, personality, and verbal style, preference is given to one of the two processes over the other.

In a well-known psychological test, children are confronted with some noun and told to utter the first verbal response that comes into their heads. In this experiment two opposite linguistic predilections are invariably exhibited: the response is intended either as a substitute for, or as a complement to the stimulus. In the latter case the stimulus and the response together form a proper syntactic construction, most usually a sentence. These two types of reaction have been labeled substitutive and predicative.

To the stimulus *hut* one response was *burnt out;* another, *is a poor little house.* Both reactions are predicative; but the first creates a purely narrative context, while in the second there is a double connection with the subject *hut*: on the one hand, a positional (namely, syntactic) contiguity, and on the other a semantic similarity.

The same stimulus produced the following substitutive reactions: the tautology *hut;* the synonyms *cabin* and *hovel;* the antonym *palace*, and the metaphors *den* and *burrow*. The capacity of two words to replace one another is an instance of positional similarity, and, in addition, all these responses are linked to the stimulus by semantic similarity (or contrast). Metonymical responses to the same stimulus, such as *thatch, litter,* or *poverty,* combine and contrast the positional similarity with semantic contiguity.

In manipulating these two kinds of connection (similarity and contiguity) in both their aspects (positional and semantic) – selecting, combining, and ranking them – an individual exhibits his personal style, his verbal predilections and preferences.

In verbal art the interaction of these two elements is especially pronounced. Rich material for the study of this relationship is to be found in verse patterns which require a compulsory parallelism between adjacent lines, for example in Biblical poetry or in the West Finnic and, to some extent, the Russian oral traditions. This provides an objective criterion of what in the given speech community acts as a correspondence. Since on any verbal level – morphemic, lexical, syntactic, and phraseological – either of these two relations (similarity and contiguity) can appear – and each in either of two aspects –, an impressive range of possible configurations is created. Either of the two gravitational poles may prevail. In Russian lyrical songs, for example, metaphoric constructions predominate, while in the heroic epics the metonymic way is preponderant.

In poetry there are various motives which determine the choice between these alternants. The primacy of the metaphoric process in the literary schools of romanticism and symbolism has been repeatedly acknowledged, but it is still insufficiently realized that it is the predominance of metonymy which underlies and actually predetermines the so-called "realistic" trend, which belongs to an intermediary stage between the decline of romanticism and the rise of symbolism and is opposed to both. Following the path of contiguous relationships, the realistic author metonymically digresses from the plot to the atmosphere and from the characters to the setting in space and time. He is fond of synecdochic details. In the scene of Anna Karenina's suicide Tolstoj's artistic attention is focused on the heroine's handbag; and in *War and Peace* the synecdoches "hair on the upper lip" or "bare shoulders" are used by the same writer to stand for the female characters to whom these features belong.

The alternative predominance of one or the other of these two processes is by no means confined to verbal art. The same oscillation occurs in sign systems other than language.[24] A salient example from the history of painting is the manifestly metonymical orientation of cubism, where the object is transformed into a set of synecdoches; the surrealist painters responded with a patently metaphorical attitude. Ever since the productions of D. W. Griffith, the art of the cinema, with its highly developed capacity for changing the angle, perspective and focus of "shots", has broken with the tradition of the theater and ranged an unprecedented variety of synecdochic "close-ups" and metonymic "set-ups" in general. In such pictures as those of Charlie Chaplin, these devices in turn were superseded by a novel, metaphoric "montage" with its "lap dissolves" – the filmic similes.[25]

The bipolar structure of language (or other semiotic systems), and, in aphasia, the fixation on one of these poles to the exclusion

---

[24]   I ventured a few sketchy remarks on the metonymical turn in verbal art ('Pro realizm u mystectvi,' *Vaplite*, Kharkov, 1927, No. 2; 'Randbemerkungen zur Prosa des Dichters Pasternak,' *Slavische Rundschau*, VII, 1935), in painting ('Futurizm,' *Iskusstvo*, Moscow, Aug. 2, 1919) and in motion pictures ('Úpadek filmu,' *Listy pro umění a kritiku*, I, Prague, 1933), but the crucial problem of the two polar processes awaits a detailed investigation.

[25]   Cf. B. Balazs, *Theory of the film* (London, 1952).

of the other require systematic comparative study. The retention of either of these alternatives in the two types of aphasia must be confronted with the predominance of the same pole in certain styles, personal habits, current fashions, etc. A careful analysis and comparison of these phenomena with the whole syndrome of the corresponding type of aphasia is an imperative task for joint research by experts in psychopathology, psychology, linguistics, poetics, and semiotic, the general science of signs. The dichotomy here discussed appears to be of primal significance and consequence for all verbal behavior and for human behavior in general.[26]

To indicate the possibilities of the projected comparative research, we choose an example from a Russian folktale which employs parallelism as a comic device: "Thomas is a bachelor; Jeremiah is unmarried" (*Fomá xólost; Erjóma neženát*). Here the predicates in the two parallel clauses are associated by similarity: they are in fact synonymous. The subjects of both clauses are masculine proper names and hence morphologically similar, while on the other hand they denote two contiguous heroes of the same tale, created to perform identical actions and thus to justify the use of synonymous pairs of predicates. A somewhat modified version of the same construction occurs in a familiar wedding song in which each of the wedding guests is addressed in turn by his first name and patronymic: "Gleb is a bachelor; Ivanovič is unmarried." While both predicates here are again synonyms, the relationship between the two subjects is changed: both are proper names denoting the same man and are normally used contiguously as a mode of polite address.

In the quotation from the folk tale the two parallel clauses refer to two separate facts, the marital status of Thomas and the similar status of Jeremiah. In the verse from the wedding song, however, the two clauses are synonymous: they redundantly reiterate the

[26] For the psychological and sociological aspects of this dichotomy see Bateson's views on "progressional" and "selective integration" and Parsons' on the "conjunction-disjunction dichotomy" in children's development: J. Ruesch and G. Bateson, *Communication, the social matrix of psychiatry* (New York, 1951), pp. 183ff.; T. Parsons and R. F. Bales, *Family, socialization and interaction process* (Glencoe, 1955), pp. 119f.

celibacy of the same hero, splitting him into two verbal hypostases.

The Russian novelist Gleb Ivanovič Uspenskij (1840–1902) in the last years of his life suffered from a mental illness involving a speech disorder. His first name and patronymic, *Gleb Ivanovič*, traditionally combined in polite intercourse, for him split into two distinct names designating two separate beings: Gleb was endowed with all his virtues, while Ivanovič, the name relating the son to the father, became the incarnation of all Uspenskij's vices. The linguistic aspect of this split personality is the patient's inability to use two symbols for the same thing, and it is thus a similarity disorder. Since the similarity disorder is bound up with the metonymical bent, an examination of the literary manner Uspenskij had employed as a young writer takes on particular interest. And the study of Anatolij Kamegulov, who analyzed Uspenskij's style, bears out our theoretical expectations. He shows that Uspenskij had a particular penchant for metonymy, and especially for synecdoche, and that he carried it so far that "the reader is crushed by the multiplicity of detail unloaded on him in a limited verbal space, and is physically unable to grasp the whole, so that the portrait is often lost."[27]

To be sure, the metonymical style in Uspenskij is obviously prompted by the prevailing literary canon of his time, late nineteenth-century "realism"; but the personal stamp of Gleb Ivanovič made his pen particularly suitable for this artistic trend in its extreme manifestations and finally left its mark upon the verbal aspect of his mental illness.

A competition between both devices, metonymic and metaphoric, is manifest in any symbolic process, either intrapersonal or social.

---

[27] A. Kamegulov, *Stil' Gleba Uspenskogo* (Leningrad, 1930), pp. 65, 145. One of such disintegrated portraits cited by the monograph: "From underneath an ancient straw cap with a black spot on its shield, there peeked two braids resembling the tusks of a wild boar; a chin grown fat and pendulous definitively spread over the greasy collars of the calico dicky and in thick layer lay on the coarse collar of the canvas coat, firmly buttoned on the neck. From below this coat to the eyes of the observer there protruded massive hands with a ring, which had eaten into the fat finger, a cane with a copper top, a significant bulge of the stomach and the presence of very broad pants, almost of muslin quality, in the broad ends of which hid the toes of the boots."

Thus in an inquiry into the structure of dreams, the decisive question is whether the symbols and the temporal sequences used are based on contiguity (Freud's metonymic "displacement" and synecdochic "condensation") or on similarity (Freud's "identification and symbolism").[28] The principles underlying magic rites have been resolved by Frazer into two types: charms based on the law of similarity and those founded on association by contiguity. The first of these two great branches of sympathetic magic has been called "homoeopathic" or "imitative", and the second, "contagious magic".[29] This bipartition is indeed illuminating. Nonetheless, for the most part, the question of the two poles is still neglected, despite its wide scope and importance for the study of any symbolic behavior, especially verbal, and of its impairments. What is the main reason for this neglect?

Similarity in meaning connects the symbols of a metalanguage with the symbols of the language referred to. Similarity connects a metaphorical term with the term for which it is substituted. Consequently, when constructing a metalanguage to interpret tropes, the researcher possesses more homogeneous means to handle metaphor, whereas metonymy, based on a different principle, easily defies interpretation. Therefore nothing comparable to the rich literature on metaphor[30] can be cited for the theory of metonymy. For the same reason, it is generally realized that romanticism is closely linked with metaphor, whereas the equally intimate ties of realism with metonymy usually remain unnoticed. Not only the tool of the observer but also the object of observation is responsible for the preponderance of metaphor over metonymy in scholarship. Since poetry is focused upon sign, and pragmatical prose primarily upon referent, tropes and figures were studied mainly as poetical devices. The principle of similarity underlies poetry; the metrical parallelism of lines or the phonic equivalence of rhyming words prompts the question of semantic similarity and

[28]   S. Freud, *Die Traumdeutung*, 9th ed. (Vienna, 1950).
[29]   J. G. Frazer, *The golden bough: A study in magic and religion*, Part I, 3rd ed. (Vienna, 1950), chapter III.
[30]   C. F. P. Stutterheim, *Het begrip metaphoor* (Amsterdam, 1941).

contrast; there exist, for instance, grammatical and anti-grammatical but never agrammatical rhymes. Prose, on the contrary, is forwarded essentially by contiguity. Thus, for poetry, metaphor, and for prose, metonymy is the line of least resistance and, consequently, the study of poetical tropes is directed chiefly toward metaphor. The actual bipolarity has been artificially replaced in these studies by an amputated, unipolar scheme which, strikingly enough, coincides with one of the two aphasic patterns, namely with the contiguity disorder.[31]

[31]   Thanks are due to Hugh McLean for his valuable assistance and to Justinia Besharov for her original observations on tropes and figures.

SUPPLEMENT

SELECTED LIST OF STUDIES IN GENERAL PHONOLOGY
(1931–1955)

M. J. ANDRADE, 'Some questions of fact and policy concerning phonemes,' *Language*, XII (1936).

O. AXMANOVA, *Fonologija* (Moscow, 1954).

C. E. BAZELL, 'The choice of criteria in structural linguistics,' *Word*, X (1954).

B. BLOCH, 'A set of postulates for phonemic analysis,' *Language*, XXV (1948).

L. BLOOMFIELD, *Language* (New York, 1933). Chapters V–VIII.

E. BUYSSENS, 'Mise au point de quelques notions fondamentales de la phonologie,' *Cahiers Ferdinand de Saussure*, VIII (1949).

J. CAMARA, *Principios de Linguistica Geral* (Rio de Janeiro, 1954). Chapters II–III.

Y. R. CHAO, 'The non-uniqueness of phonemic solution of phonetic systems,' Academica Sinica, Institute of History and Philology, *Bulletin*, IV (Shanghai, 1934).

E. C. CHERRY, M. HALLE, R. JAKOBSON, 'Toward the logical description of languages in their phonemic aspect,' *Language*, XXIX (1953).

E. COSERIU, W. VASQUES, *Para la unificacion de las sciencias fonicas* (Montevideo, 1953).

E. DIETH, *Vademecum der Phonetik* (Bern, 1950). Chapter III C.

B. FADDEGON, 'Phonetics and phonology, '*Meded. Kon. Nederl. Akad. Wetensch.*, Afd. Letterkunde, II (1938).

E. FISCHER-JØRGENSEN, 'Phonologie,' *Archiv für vergleichende Phonetik*, V (1941); 'On the definition of phoneme categories on a distributional basis,' *Acta Linguistica*, VII (1952).

H. FREI, 'Langue, parole et différenciation,' *Journal de Psychologie* (1952).

C. C. FRIES, K. L. PIKE, 'Coexistent phonemic systems,' *Language*, XXV (1949).

A. W. DE GROOT, 'Neutralisation d'oppositions,' *Neophilologus*, XXV (1940).

M. HALLE, 'The strategy of phonemics,' *Word*, X (1954).

Z. S. HARRIS, *Methods in structural linguistics* (Chicago, 1951); 'From phoneme to morpheme,' *Language*, XXXI (1955).

L. HJELMSLEV, 'Über die Beziehungen der Phonetik zur Sprachwissenschaft,' *Archiv für vergleichende Phonetik*, II (1938).

C. F. HOCKETT, 'A manual of phonology' = *Indiana University Publications in Anthropology and Linguistics*, XI (1955).

R. JAKOBSON, 'The phonemic and grammatical aspects of language in their interrelations,' *Actes du Sixième Congrès International des Linguistes* (Paris, 1949).

R. JAKOBSON, C. G. M. FANT, M. HALLE, *Preliminaries to speech analysis*, third printing (Massachusetts Institute of Technology, Acoustics Laboratory, 1955).

D. JONES, *The phoneme: its nature and use* (Cambridge, 1950).

A. G. JUILLAND, 'A bibliography of diachronic phonemics,' *Word*, IX (1953), pp. 198–208.

J. M. KOŘÍNEK, *Úvod do jazykospytu* (Bratislava, 1948). Chapter II.

E. KRUISINGA, 'Fonetiek en fonologie,' *Taal en Leven*, VI (1943).

J. V. LAZICZIUS, 'Probleme der Phonologie,' *Ungarische Jahrbücher*, XV (1935).

E. A. LLORACH, *Fonologia Española* (Madrid, 1954). Primera parte: fonologia general.

A. MARTINET, *Phonology as functional phonetics* (London. 1949); 'Où en est la phonologie?' *Lingua*, I (1949).

K. L. PIKE, *Phonemics: a technique for reducing languages to writing* (Ann Arbor, 1947); *Tone languages* (Ann Arbor, 1948); 'Grammatical prerequisites to phonemic analysis,' *Word*, III (1947); 'More on grammatical prerequisites,' *Word*, VIII (1952); *Language in relation to a unified theory of the structure of human behavior*, II (Glendale, Cal., 1955).

M. POLAK, 'Fonetiek en fonologie,' *Levende Talen* (1940)

H. J. POS, 'Phonologie en betekenisleer' = *Mededeelingen der Koninklijke Nederlandsche Akademie van Wetenschappen*, Afd. Letterkunde. NR, No. 13 (1938).

E. SAPIR, *Selected writings* (Berkeley and Los Angeles, 1949), pp. 7–60.

E. SEIDEL, *Das Wesen der Phonologie* (Bucharest-Copenhagen, 1943).

A. SOTAVALTA, 'Die Phonetik und ihre Beziehungen zu den Grenzwissenschaften' = *Annales Academiae Scientiarum Fennicae*, XXXI, No. 3 (1936).

R. H. STETSON, *Motor phonetics* (Amsterdam, 1951).

M. SWADESH, 'The phonemic principle,' *Language*, X (1934).

B. TRNKA, 'Určování fonému,' *Acta Universitatis Carolinae* (Prague, 1954).

N. TRUBETZKOY, *Principes de phonologie* (Paris, 1949). German text: 'Grundzüge der Phonologie' = *Travaux du Cercle Linguistique de Prague*, VII (1939).

W. F. TWADDELL, 'On defining the phoneme' = Supplement to *Language*, XVI (1935); 'Stetson's model and the <supra-segmental phonemes>,' *Language*, XXIX (1935).

N. VAN WIJK, *Phonologie: een hoofdstuk uit de structurele taalwetenschap* (The Hague, 1939). A substantially revised version is·being prepared by A. Reichling.

E. ZWIRNER, 'L'opposition phonologique et la variation des phonèmes,'
Archiv für vergleichende Phonetik, II (1938); 'Phonologie und Phonetik,'
Acta Linguistica, I (1939).

DISCUSSIONS

Akademija Nauk SSSR, Otdelenie literatury i jazyka, *Izvestija*, XI (1952)
and XII (1953) – Diskussija po voprosam fonologii.
International Congresses of Phonetic Sciences, *Proceedings*, I–III (1933,
1935, 1938).
Journal of the Acoustical Society of America, XXII (1950) – Proceedings
of the Speech Communication Conference at MIT; XXIV (1952) –
Conference on Speech Analysis.
Travaux du Cercle Linguistique de Copenhague, V (1949) – Recherches
structurales.
Travaux du Cercle Linguistique de Prague, IV (1931) – Réunion phonologique internationale tenue à Prague; VIII (1939) – Etudes phono-
logiques. dédiées à la mémoire de N. S. Trubetzkoy.

CPSIA information can be obtained
at www.ICGtesting.com
Printed in the USA
BVHW060844010219
539210BV00002B/532/P

9 781333 795658